The Political Economy of Contemporary Spain

The so-called 'Spanish miracle', beginning in the mid-1990s, eventually became a nightmare for the majority of the population, culminating in the present-day economic and political crisis. This book explores the main features of the Spanish political-economic model during both the growth and crisis periods.

Analyzing the causes and consequences of the continuing economic crisis in Spain, this book delves into five analytical axes: the evolution of the growth model; the role of Spain in the international division of labor; the financial sector and its influence on the rest of the economy; changes in the labor market; and the distributional consequences of both the expansive phase and the later crisis. Furthermore, contributors examine the formation of a triangle of actors (the government sector, building sector, and financial capital) that shaped the Spanish growth model, together with the effects of Spain's membership in the Economic and Monetary Union. Also considering ecological problems, gender issues, and the immigration question, this book challenges the alleged recovery of living conditions during recent years, as well as the explanation of the crisis as the result of irrational behaviors or the greedy nature of certain actors.

The Political Economy of Contemporary Spain provides a coherent explanation of the Spanish economic crisis based on a pluralistic approach, while proposing several measures that could contribute to a transformation of Spain's economic and social models.

Luis Buendía is Assistant Professor of Public Economics and Political Economy at the University of León, Spain. Since 2014, he has taken part in a project on the crisis in Southern Europe, financed by the Sheffield Political Economy Research Institute, and he has also been a member of the Steering Committee of the Asociación de Economía Crítica (Critical Economics Association).

Ricardo Molero-Simarro is Honorary Fellow at the Department of Applied Economics I (International Economics and Development) of the Complutense University of Madrid, Spain. He has also been a researcher at the School of Oriental and African Studies, UK, and the Peking University, China. His lines of research include aspects of income inequality, as well as monetary systems. In 2014, he was invited as a speaker to the Labour Economics after the Crisis Conference organized by the European Commission.

Routledge Frontiers of Political Economy

For a full list of titles in this series please visit www.routledge.com/books/series/ SE0345

The Political Economy of Contemporary Spain

From Miracle to Mirage

**Edited by Luis Buendía and
Ricardo Molero-Simarro**

Routledge
Taylor & Francis Group

LONDON AND NEW YORK

First published 2018 by Routledge

2 Park Square, Milton Park, Abingdon, Oxfordshire OX14 4RN
52 Vanderbilt Avenue, New York, NY 10017

Routledge is an imprint of the Taylor & Francis Group, an informa business

First issued in paperback 2020

British Library Cataloguing-in-Publication Data
A catalogue record for this book is available from the British Library

Library of Congress Cataloging-in-Publication Data
A catalog record for this book has been requested

ISBN: 978-1-138-30571-7 (hbk)
ISBN: 978-0-367-59274-5 (pbk)

Typeset in Times New Roman
by Apex CoVantage, LLC

To our mothers.
We owe it all to you.

Contents

Figures

Tables

Contributors

Luis Buendía is Assistant Professor at the Department of Economics and Statistics of the University of León (Spain).

Eduardo Garzón Espinosa is a PhD candidate at the Department of Applied Economics I (International Economy and Development) of the Complutense University of Madrid (Spain).

Manuel Gracia holds a PhD in Economics and he is Researcher at the Instituto Complutense de Estudios Internacionales (ICEI) of the Complutense University of Madrid (Spain).

Juan Pablo Mateo is Visiting Scholar at PACE University (Pleasantville, New York, USA) and Assistant Professor at the University of Valladolid (Spain).

Bibiana Medialdea García is Interim Associate Professor at the Department of Applied Economics I (International Economy and Development) of the Complutense University of Madrid (Spain).

Ricardo Molero-Simarro is Honorary Fellow at the Department of Applied Economics I (International Economy and Development) of the Complutense University of Madrid (Spain).

Miguel Montanyà Revuelto holds a PhD in Economics and he is a Researcher at the Complutense University of Madrid and Lecturer at the Isabel I University (Spain).

F. Javier Murillo Arroyo is Adjunct Professor at the Department of Applied Economics I (International Economy and Development) of the Complutense University of Madrid (Spain).

María José Paz is currently Lecturer and Researcher at the Department of Applied Economics I (International Economy and Development) of the Complutense University of Madrid (Spain).

María Eugenia Ruiz-Gálvez holds a PhD in Economics from the Complutense University of Madrid and she is Researcher at the Instituto Complutense de Estudios Internacionales (ICEI) (Spain).

Antonio Sanabria Martín is Adjunct Professor at the Department of Applied Economics I (International Economy and Development) of the Complutense University of Madrid (Spain).

Lucía Vicent Valverde holds a PhD in Economics from the Complutense University of Madrid and he is Researcher at the Instituto Complutense de Estudios Internacionales (ICEI) and FUHEM-Ecosocial (Spain).

Introduction

The political economy of the Spanish growth model and its structural adjustment process

Luis Buendía and Ricardo Molero-Simarro[1]

This book is the main outcome of a research project whose origin traces back to 2005, when most of the authors began to analyze the causes, nature, and consequences of the structural adjustment programs and policies adopted in Latin America and the United States, using a social-class standpoint. Those adjustments adopted different forms depending on the country. In previous work, we studied that adjustment process in six countries (Argentina, Brazil, Bolivia, Guatemala, Venezuela, and the United States), from the beginning of the 1980s to the mid-2000s. The results of our research were published in Álvarez et al. (2008, 2009, 2011).

The starting point for our research was the notion that adjustment processes focus on wages, in the sense that they seek to cheapen the labor force, as well as to achieve redistribution of the socially generated economic surplus, in order to counteract a crisis in the profitability of capital in effect worldwide since the 1970s (Sanabria, 2009: 29; see also Harvey, 2005). To be sure, the goal of adjustment policies has been to push down labor costs (direct and indirect) and consequently to transfer income from labor to capital, with the aim of recovering profit margins across the world economy.

Wages are compensation for labor. However, wage is not considered here as just an exclusively monetary variable, but also as a social relationship that involves three distinct aspects or components of the distribution of economic surplus (on this we follow the Marxist tradition as stated, for instance, and with varying approaches in Mandel, 1967: Ch. 3; Gouverneur, 1983: Ch. XV; or more recently, Vasapollo, 2012: Ch. 12): the direct wage (payment for completion of a certain job); the indirect wage (social services and transfers in kind that imply a guarantee of access to basic services such as housing, health, education, dependency care, and so on, to be covered by the state through that part of the public expense classified as social spending); and the deferred wage (monetary transfers received when working life is interrupted, either temporarily, in the case of unemployment benefits or sick-leave compensation, or permanently, in the case of retirement pensions).

These three dimensions of the wage relationship have all been affected by adjustment processes. In 1995, Sebastian Edwards, a former World Bank Chief Economist for Latin America and the Caribbean, published an influential book entitled *Crisis and Reform in Latin America: From Despair to Hope* (Edwards, 1995), in which he proposed five dimensions in order to test the implementation of adjustment policies: fiscal adjustment, trade liberalization, financial market reforms, privatization, and labor market deregulation. All of the countries analyzed in our prior research adhered, to a greater or lesser extent, to the adjustment policies prescribed for these five dimensions:

i) Fiscal adjustment: budgetary balance has been achieved through increasing revenue, but also, and to a greater extent, through cuts in public spending, in order to both reduce the presence of the state in economic activity and, concerning social expenditures, 'make work more attractive'.

ii) Trade liberalization: the reduction of tariffs and other barriers to international trade has increased the exposure of national economies to international competition in such a way that local producers have faced increasing pressure on their margins.

iii) Financial market reforms: free entry of foreign capital into these countries has been permitted in an attempt to attract not only foreign direct investment (FDI) to national strategic sectors, but also other capital flows to domestic financial markets.

iv) Privatization: the sale of public enterprises has caused the state to withdraw from potentially profitable activities, thus opening new spaces for private capital accumulation.

v) Labor market deregulation: a series of measures to facilitate hiring and firing have hindered the ability of workers to collectively bargain on their working conditions and, subsequently, declining worker compensation has provided a more favorable environment for profitability.

Our conclusions published in Álvarez et al. (2009) were that adjustment affected mainly wages (understood in their broadest sense, including direct real wages as well as indirect and deferred wages); that adjustment had a worldwide scope (in peripheral as well as core countries); and that its duration was permanent (not limited to adjustment packages imposed by international financial institutions).

Following these arguments, we contend that the crisis that the world economy has endured in recent years has its origins in the neoliberal economic model that emerged during the 1970s. This model was based on a process of permanent structural adjustment on wages as a basis for the recovery of corporate profitability. Although this process, which has caused a progressive pauperization of the working class, allowed for a relative recovery of global economic growth, it has proved to have intrinsic limits (Howard and King, 2008; Callinicos, 2012). Thus the accumulation of significant tensions in the economic sphere set off a financial-speculative bubble that put into question the viability of the neoliberal model (Vasapollo, 2012; *pace* Duménil and Lévy, 2011). Nevertheless, responses to the crisis have been made on the basis of a reaffirmation of the wage adjustment process. As a consequence, the way out of the crisis has been seen to rely on an intensification of the contradictions of the neoliberal model (Boyer, 2012; Palley, 2013).

In this book, we analyze thus the current crisis in Spain as a part of a broader process whose origins can be also found in the worldwide crisis of the late 1960s and the 1970s. In examining the case of Spain, our main goal is to understand the causes, nature, and consequences of the current crisis. Considering that the crisis in Spain and other European countries has emerged (as in some American economies) in the context of a permanent adjustment on wages, as experienced during recent decades, the policies implemented have been a part thereof; as such, they are linked to the structural mechanisms of the economy. Concretely, we consider that the adjustment policies implemented in Spain, at least since approval of the Maastricht Treaty and reinforced from 2009 onward, are a part of the expansion of the overall adjustment process to a worldwide scale, with causes rooted in the structural functioning of the economy (see also Greer, 2014; Hermann, 2016).

Our analysis takes a critical approach in which we combine several heterodox perspectives. Following a general historical-structural strategy, the book disentangles the links between production, finance, and distribution both before and after the crisis, but in our own version of Harcourt's 'horses for courses' approach (Harcourt, 1999), we use different analytical approaches in the study of each of those spheres. Although the Marxist toolbox (as applied by Shaikh, 2016) is our choice to understand the growth pattern, the study of commercial and productive external insertion draw on a core–periphery approach (originally based in the works by Prebisch, 1962, but adding contributions by Hopkins and Wallerstein, 1977, or Gereffi and Korzeniewick, 1994). In addition, Minsky (1992) and Keen (2011) are the main theoretical references to address the process of indebtedness and increasing financial fragility of the Spanish economy. The analysis of labor market and income distribution starts from the consideration that the evolution thereof is reliant on (and is functional to) the trends examined in the rest of the book. Concretely, with the aim of enhancing external competitiveness, reducing public debt, and restoring corporate profitability, the labor market has been deregulated while the welfare state has been eroded. This has led to the decrease of relative wages and to an increase of inequality in its different dimensions.

In empirical terms, our starting point is the mid-1990s (*ca.* 1995), in order to study how the so-called 'Spanish miracle' eventually became a nightmare for the majority of the population, and continues then to the present, as we attempt to elucidate the real reasons behind the indebtedness of the Spanish economy. In this sense, our analysis (and all the chapters included in this book) covers both the last expansive cycle (1996–2007) and the phase of crisis and adjustment (2008–2015) in each of the analytical areas on which we have divided our study. This Introduction completes our work by linking those analytical strategies under the previously mentioned historical-structural approach and by setting out the political economic logic of those two recent periods in the progression of Spain's economy.

The political economy of the Spanish growth model (1995–2007)

Only two political parties have formed the government of Spain during most of its democratic period, which began in 1978 (with the initial exception of the first term, until 1982, when a different center party held power). Those two parties are the conservative Partido Popular (PP) and the social democratic Partido Socialista Obrero Español (PSOE). As has been the case elsewhere in Europe, as social democracy moderated its positions, the differences in economic policy making between those two parties became decreasingly significant. As a consequence, the PSOE had already by the 1980s given up on attempts to implement countercyclical policies, embracing the monetarist consensus that prioritized inflation targeting over any other economic goal (Pérez, 1999: 671).

Probably more important for the specialization of the economy was the emergence of political consensus around the building sector, which became key for the growth model. That sector had also been highly important under the Francoist dictatorship, but during the expansive phase of 1996–2007 it became more relevant, inasmuch as both parties (the PP and the PSOE) had strong incentives to support it. In effect, the dependence of the economy on that sector for the creation of employment (and thereby extraordinary public revenues) conditioned public policies in favor of the building sector. This sector was at the center of the growth model, as it was able to meet both private demand (housing) and public demand (large infrastructures and even public services when they were outsourced). This sector was densely concentrated around a group of just six construction firms with close links to political power (see Recio et al. 2006; López and Rodríguez, 2010: 323–331).

In addition to the government sector (as key facilitator) and the building sector, a third actor was central to the political economy of the growth model: financial capital. In Spain, the financial sector had traditionally been formed by three kinds of institutions: banks, savings banks, and credit unions, with the former two accounting for over 95% of deposits. The difference between banks and savings banks is that the latter had traditionally been closer in their mode of operation to quasi-public institutions, having more social concerns than banks, which are conventional private-sector institutions. However, since the financial reforms at the beginning of the 1980s the differences between these two types of institutions have eroded. Moreover, as financial capital got more concentrated, it became a very powerful actor, and policies applied in the 1980s by social democratic governments privileged their position to the detriment of industrial capital or even government accounts (Pérez, 1999).

During the expansive phase, financial firms saw their profit margins increase as a consequence of the combination of membership in the Economic and Monetary Union (EMU) (which pushed down interest rates) and expanding demand for mortgages. At the same time, the political parties in power (mainly the PP and the PSOE) exerted control over savings banks by appointing their principal managers, allowing the parties to finance large infrastructure projects in order to gain electoral support. This made Spain the country with the longest high-capacity road networks and high-speed rail network, even in a context of no actual demand. Despite the increase in stations with no significant traffic and their ecological impact, these projects were absolutely functional for the growth model (López and Rodríguez, 2010: 326–330).

We can thus see the formation of a triangle of actors in key decision-making positions to shape the growth model. Their decisions were legitimized election after election, which itself points to a quandary that requires explanation; but before exploring this, it is necessary to examine more closely the workings of the whole economy through each of its main components.

Between 1996 and 2007, Spain achieved one of the fastest growth rates of the entire European Union (EU), at an annual 3.7%. As explained in Chapter 1, this growth was based on an accumulation of factors (i.e., labor and capital). Concerning capital, residential investment caused residential capital to grow faster than productive capital, whereas technological investment was weaker at the end of the period than at the beginning. If 32.6% of investment in 1996 was allocated to residential ends and 21.3% to machinery, the respective figures in 2007 were 40% and 16% (FBBVA, 2014; see also Mateo and Montanyà, 2014). The share of construction in the gross domestic product (GDP) thus rose from 8.6% in 1995 to 10.4% in 2007 (data from the Spanish Statistical Office, INE). It comes as no surprise that these trends led to a decrease in labor productivity, particularly in certain sectors, as shown in Chapter 1. With respect to labor, it must be noted that Spain accounted for one of three jobs created in the EU during this period, earning the country's economic performance the nickname 'the Spanish miracle'. This increase in the demand for labor was largely met by a huge increase in the supply of foreign labor: between 1996 and 2009, the percentage of foreigners in the labor force increased from 1.2% to 14.1%. Those immigrants came increasingly from Latin America and found jobs with worsening conditions: lower wages, greater incidence of temporariness, longer working hours, and greater presence in the shadow economy (Aragón et al., 2010).

This investment-intensive pattern of growth also required major sources of financing, which could come either from domestic or foreign savings. Analysis of Spain's balance of payments shows that such funds also came to Spain from abroad. The current account balance turned to deficit as consumption and, thereby imports, rapidly increased. Spain's balance of goods has traditionally been in deficit, and this was formerly compensated by a surplus in the balance of services due to revenues from tourism. However, since the end of the 1990s, the surplus in services proved insufficient and the net lending position of the economy worsened. By 2007, net borrowing was equal to 9.6% of GDP (CES, 2012). This was the consequence of increasing domestic demand, but also of a worsening of Spain's external insertion, with Spanish exports tending toward products with lower added value.

Explanation for these trends is related also to the integration of Spain into the EU, which has emphasized the dependent external insertion of the economy both in inter- and intra-industry terms. On the one hand, the trade pattern of Spain is mainly intra-industry, as is the case with many EU countries. However, imports, even when belonging to the same industry as exports, have lower technological content than the latter and are therefore cheaper. As a consequence, the coverage rate (measured as the ratio of exports to imports) was at 0.85 in 1998, but 0.65 in 2007. This means that whereas core EU countries were able to make the most of their trade advantages, EU periphery countries (including Spain) suffered increasing imbalances. This lack of competitiveness has indeed been structural in nature, but until Spain entered the EMU, such problems tended to be addressed through currency devaluation. When devaluation is no longer an option, another method is required for financing such imbalances, and the alternatives are either through FDI or through borrowing. After Spain entered the EMU (and here we have another line of influence from Spain's integration into the EU), the country became an attractive destination for FDI. This has led to a situation in which foreign capital has acquired control positions of some strategic sectors, which has subordinated the pattern of specialization of the Spanish economy to the interests of some transnational companies, thus reinforcing the dependent role of Spain in the international division of labor (as shown in Chapter 2).

Data from Eurostat show notwithstanding that, rather than FDI, the main source of financing during 1996–2007 was borrowing and the issuance of financial instruments (Garzón, 2013). And here we have a third aspect related to EU integration: had Spain not been a member of the EU, it would have had a harder time borrowing, and that borrowing would have been more expensive.

In any case, as a result of the inward flow of funds, borrowing in Spain became huge, and by 2009, the overall debt was estimated to be 502% of GDP (Lapavitsas et al., 2010). As we will see in Chapter 3, this debt was not all foreign debt, but even domestic debt had its origins in borrowing by Spanish banks conducted abroad. Worth noting is that most of this debt belonged to the private sector. Indeed, private-sector debt, at around 90% of GDP by 1994, reached 312% of GDP in 2007 (data from Sanabria and Medialdea, 2014).[2]

The role of the financial sector was thus essential. Given that interest rates were going down as a result of membership in the EMU, financial institutions adopted an extensive strategy: credit provision grew at 30% per year in the final segment of the expansive phase. Domestic savings, and thereby deposits, were not growing as quickly, so banks were obliged to borrow in international markets. Concretely, banks were borrowing over a quarter of their balance sheets from their German and Dutch counterparts (Fernández-Villaverde and Ohanian, 2010: 10). Those funds were channeled to the building sector: credit allocated thereto grew by 15.7% yearly between 1995 and 2007 (Molero, 2014). The financial sector was therefore functional to the pattern of specialization, and the reliance on the building sector compounded vulnerability because credit delinquency in that sector was especially high when the crisis started.

Meanwhile, the public sector became a facilitator of the whole process. Compared to the rest of EMU countries, Spain has suffered from underdevelopment of its public sector in terms of both public expenditures and government revenues (measured as the percentage of GDP). Even in the final part of the expansive phase, when revenues reached an all-time high, they were still 4 percentage points lower than the Eurozone average. In spite of its relatively small size, Spain fulfilled its Maastricht commitment, and both public deficit and public debt were reduced: by 2007, it was among the EU countries with the lowest public debt to GDP ratio.

However, more important than its size was the public sector's role in economic policy making. Already by the 1980s, as mentioned, the public sector was actively privileging the interests of financial capital in a way that harmed industrial capital. This retreat from any kind of industrial policy (which, in the absence also of a national enterprising bourgeoisie, reinforced Spain's subordinate external insertion) went further in the 1990s with an extensive program of privatizations. To this was added another program of deregulation affecting several realms, including the financial sector and the construction and real estate sectors. In the case of the latter, the governments aimed at eliminating any obstacle to its expansion: in 1998, a new law on building permits allowed for construction almost anywhere. At the same time, other aspects that acted as incentives to the construction sector included a reduction in the stock of public housing and the long-lasting policy of tax relief for home buying, as well as a 'lax environmental policy . . . and subsidies for squandering energy and water on inefficient property developments' (López and Rodríguez, 2011b), which have contributed to the ecological unsustainability of the Spanish growth model (see Carpintero, 2005).

Meanwhile, the state neglected its role as income redistributor, a topic we deal with in Chapter 5. Regarding the revenue side, Spain over the last two decades acquired one of the highest nominal tax rates in the Organisation for Economic Co-operation and Development (OECD), despite which fiscal pressure (and thereby effective tax rates) fell to well below the average (data from OECD.Stat). This problem was never addressed. On the contrary, the expansive phase was used to make the tax system more fragile, as public revenues became more and more dependent on the real estate sector. Estimates from the IMF (2009) show that the increase in such revenues after 1995 was mainly cyclical, and a great portion of new revenues (between 2.5 and 3.0 percentage points of GDP) was due to the real estate sector. Furthermore, according to Zack et al. (2013), had it not been for the effect of asset revaluation in the improvement in tax revenues, the tax balance would have already registered a deficit in 2004. All this notwithstanding, administrations from both the PP and the PSOE prioritized tax cuts in their respective tax policies, with a reduction in the number of tax brackets and marginal rates in income taxes, the elimination of wealth taxes, and the reduction of inheritance taxes (Muñoz de Bustillo and Antón, 2014).

With respect to the expenditure side of government accounts, Spain has traditionally suffered from 'social underdevelopment' (Navarro, 2006). The extraordinary revenues of the period were used to reduce the tax burden instead of trying to tackle that underdevelopment in a systematic way. Therefore, although it is true that during the expansive phase some universal features were amplified, at the same time, certain cutbacks and privatizations were applied as a part of the consolidation process of public expenditures (Rodríguez Cabrero, 2011; Moreno, 2012). Using the expression of Muñoz de Bustillo and Antón (2014), the Spanish welfare state turned back before arriving at the level of its European partners. This in turn had a clear effect on inequalities, which helps elucidate the ironies stemming from the process.

Two questions remain unanswered so far. First, if the economy was enjoying healthy rates of growth and creation of employment was so astonishing, how is it that domestic savings were too low to meet the demand for investment? The second question is related to the labor share of GDP: between 1996 and 2007, the wage share of GDP at factor cost went down from 65.0% to 62.2% (data from AMECO). How could this happen in a context in which jobs were growing and unemployment dropping? The answer to these questions lies in issues of distribution and, thereby, issues of power.

During the expansive phase, wages grew more slowly on average than did productivity. That means that those gains in productivity were taken by employers in the form of profits: profits grew faster than wages, which explains the decline in the wage share of GDP (see Murillo, 2010). According to theory (see Kalecki, 1943), declining unemployment should have empowered workers, but we will show in Chapter 4 that most of the jobs created were for low-skilled workers and, in significant proportion, they were precarious (one third of contracts took this form; rates of temporary employment in Spain are among the highest in the EU; Recio and Banyuls, 2004). These jobs provided lower wages, and by 2007, the in-work, at-risk-of-poverty rate was almost the same as at the beginning of the 2000s, and 2.3 points higher than the EU-15 average. Those wage levels did not help stimulate productivity in a vicious circle that is related to the peripheral position of the economy (see Chapter 2).

So whereas real wages (and income benefits from the Spanish underdeveloped welfare state) were growing very slowly, other sources of income increased much faster. In a context where GDP grew by 50% between 1997 and 2007, the price of financial assets and real estate assets increased by 150% and 250%, respectively (data from Barómetro Social de España).

The next question becomes, how could consumption be so dynamic, as mentioned earlier? The answer here depends on several factors. On the one hand, the wealth effect: workers were able to use their homes as collateral to finance their increasing consumption as housing prices were rising too quickly in the European country with the highest home ownership rate (López and Rodríguez, 2011a: 50). On the other hand, debt underlied the whole process; when basic needs are unmet by the labor market and/or the welfare state, the majority of the population must rely on debt. Debt was thus required to fuel the growth engine. And this returns us to our point of departure and the triangle of actors mentioned earlier.

In sum, the wealth effect acted as a legitimizer of a process with clear winners and (as we shall see) clear losers; and yet the latter lived behind a veil that allowed them to buy the fiction of living in an economic miracle. However, the bursting of the bubble in the wake of 2007 alerted the population to this mirage. As we discuss later, the socialization of losses implemented since 2010 has degenerated into a debt crisis, and the responses (in the form of fiscal austerity and internal wage devaluation policy) have only extended the structural stagnation of the economy, releasing the regressive potential in social terms that the previous growth model contained.

Crisis and adjustment in the Spanish economy (2008–2015)

The growth pattern that Spain followed, as we have explained, was built on so weak a foundation that it did not take long for problems to manifest. As with any other debt-based growth model, the problems appeared when the debt stopped renewing itself. In the case of Spain, two exogenous factors preceded the credit crunch. On the one hand, the bankruptcy of Lehman Brothers in 2008 dried up international credit channels; on the other, the increase in interest rates (from 0.25% to 4.25% in July 2008) made the situation harder to control. Anyway, as shown in Chapter 3, all this led to the outburst of the crisis and was due to the excessive reliance of the Spanish model on debt (Sanabria and Medialdea, 2016: 205).

When the financial sources of the current growth model failed, the model's engine, which had been the construction sector, was severely damaged. The tanking of this sector contributed to the largest job destruction in the Eurozone: 3.4 million jobs lost between 2007 and 2013 (and jobs in 2015 remained 2.7 million under pre-crisis figures).

On the other hand, whereas in 2007 the surplus in public-sector accounts equaled 2% of GDP, that turned to an 11% deficit in 2009, and it was still at a 5.1% deficit in 2015 (data from Eurostat). This was the result of a twofold process: i) public expenditures went up as a consequence of banks bailouts, automatic stabilizers (particularly due to the boost in unemployment benefit recipients), and, to a lesser extent, the implementation of expansionary policies in the beginning of the crisis; and ii) public revenues fell drastically. Spain was the EU-28 country where government revenues experienced the greatest fall at the onset of the crisis, at 6 percentage points of GDP; in 2015, public revenues remained 2.7 points below their 2007 level, and almost 7 points below the EU-28 average.

The initial economic policy against the crisis, launched by the PSOE government, was oriented towards stimulating the economy, meanwhile trying not to lay the burden of the crisis on workers. On the one hand, the government cut taxes (a €400 deduction in the personal income tax and a rapid value-added tax [VAT] refund) in order to encourage consumption and investment. On the other hand, the government tried to reinvigorate the construction sector by supporting social housing and public works channeled through the 'E Plan', with the aim of maintaining employment. Later, certain social assistance measures were also approved (mainly, a €420 subsidy for unemployed workers who had exhausted their benefits) in order to alleviate the declines in family income caused by job losses.

Soon, the bursting of the housing bubble began to affect banks and savings banks directly. This led to measures to bail out the financial sector, undertaken in parallel.

> The creation of a fund of €50 billion for the acquisition of financial assets and, three days later, a line granting guarantees for a total amount of €100 billion to cover new funding operations of credit institutions were approved in October 2009.
>
> (Seminari Taifa, 2010: 68)

More important still, in June 2009 the borrowing capacity of the Fund for Orderly Bank Restructuring (in Spanish Fondo de Reestructuración Ordenada Bancaria, FROB) was widened, up to €99 billion (*op.cit.*: 70). In addition, the EMU made available €100 billion extra, provided by the European Stability Mechanism after the Spanish financial-sector bailout was approved in June 2012, including the creation of a 'bad bank' (SAREB, by its Spanish acronym) in the memorandum of understanding signed with the Troika (see Sanabria and Garzón, 2013).

Recent data from the Bank of Spain (2016) show that between 2009 and 2015 the bailout cost as much as €61.5 billion, or 5.7% of GDP, of which only 2.7 billion have been returned. Banks paid themselves less than €8 billion, which means that the rest, which has been used for capitalization and/or nationalization of various savings banks (almost all of which were converted to commercial banks during the process), has only multiplied the public debt and again reflects the power correlation and the setting of priorities deriving therefrom (see Chapter 3).

In a context of increasing numbers of benefit recipients – in addition to the near doubling of unemployment benefit recipients, those receiving social assistance increased by 50% and old-age pensioners by 3% (+200,000) between 2007 and 2009 (data from OECD, Social Benefits Recipients) – the government tried to curb subsequent increases in public expenditures through measures that included a wage freeze and layoffs in the public sector; a (gradual) increase in the retirement age from 65 to 67; a rise in the years of contribution (from 35 to 37) required to access to the maximum old-age pension; the augmenting of the work-years used to calculate pensions (from the last 15 to the last 25 years); a hardening of requirements to access voluntary pre-retirement; the conversion, since 2013, of the retirement pension system from a defined benefit system to a defined contribution system; the decrease in medicines under public coverage (i.e., provided free or at a subsidized price); the outsourcing of several services in the healthcare sector and the erosion of its universality (by restriction of access to undocumented immigrants); rises in the price of childcare services; the elimination of education branches in some centers (such as those focused on students with special needs); increases in the pupil/teacher ratio; increased tuition fees and reduced grants; and privatizations in several sectors (including airports and lotteries) (see Banyuls and Recio, 2015). At the same time, the government increased both the VAT and income tax rates.

Overall, 'considering only the main items of expenditure on services', various estimates put the cuts in public spending on education, health, and other welfare programs 'at a minimum of €15 billion just between 2010 and 2013, which is to say an eighth of the money allocated to bail out banks' (Buendía, 2013: 41). This notwithstanding, parliamentary support from the PP and PSOE allowed for reform of the Constitution during the summer of 2011 (at a time when anti-austerity protests by so-called *indignados* had already erupted all over the country) in order to prioritize the payment of debt over any other goal. In this way, the political parties ensured the prevalence of financial capital interests (both national and European) over the interests of the vast majority of the population.

Furthermore, since 2010, fiscal austerity policies have also been accompanied by deep labor market reform (see Chapter 4). The stated aim of this reform was to adjust wages and prices (i.e., an internal devaluation process) in order to increase the external competitiveness of the economy. To accomplish this, various legislative acts (Law 35/2010, Royal Decree Law 7/2011, and Royal Decree Law 3/2012) diminished labor rights, facilitated and cheapened the dismissal of workers, and increased the bargaining power of companies by introducing an opt-out from collective bargaining agreements, giving priority to firm-level agreements over those at the sectorial level and by eliminating the automatic extension of such agreements whenever a new deal between employer organizations and trade unions is not reached.

Together with the very substantial increase in unemployment (especially affecting young people, see Ruiz-Gálvez, 2015), all these measures have pushed wages downward. Between 2010 and 2014, the INE Labor Price Index (designed to measure the temporal evolution of the price of labor) decreased by 0.7% annually. Not only that, but labor reforms have caused a sharp drop in the share of wages in GDP. Although this drop is a trend that dates back to at least the mid-1990s, since the outbreak of the current crisis, it contrasts with the situation in other European economies, where the relative wage has increased. In Spain the share of wages decreased from 63.2% of national income in 2010 to 61.3% in 2015; the Eurozone average increased from 63% to 63.2% during the same period (data from AMECO).

The strategy of internal wage devaluation has led to a reduction in labor costs, which have grown at below the Eurozone rate. However, this has not allowed the recovery of Spain's share of world exports, the value of which in 2015 (1.71%) was still lower than in 2007 (1.81%). This insensitivity of the export share to declining labor costs points to the need to consider other factors to explain the evolution of the economy's external competitiveness, as Chapter 2 does. As Gracia and Paz (2013: 6) explain, 'the export competitiveness of an economy in terms of cost is determined by its absolute advantage, rather than its comparative advantage', so if the decrease in costs does not lead to lower levels in absolute terms than those of its main competitors, it 'will not restore the absolute advantage' (see also Shaikh, 1980).

Moreover, 'the change in unit labor costs (ULC) depends not only on the labor costs but also on productivity' (*ibid.*). Indeed, the main indicator of ULC, nominal unit labor costs, is calculated as a ratio between nominal wage per employee and real productivity per worker. As we saw in the previous section, the Spanish economy has been hampered by its pattern of trade specialization in products of medium and low technological intensity, so productivity has barely improved during recent decades, making reduction of those costs more difficult (at least until the beginning of the crisis). In fact, given the substantially lower absolute level of wages enjoyed by Spain's main competitors in those branches, the commitment to wage devaluation has become a suicide strategy for the Spanish economy.

This is true not only because wage contraction has failed to stem the decline of the Spanish export share, but also because the absolute increase in exports made possible by the devaluation of wages has been ineffective in altering the pattern of specialization and in reversing the structural trade deficit of the Spanish economy.

This deficit has been reduced largely due to the fall in imports caused by declines in household consumption, government spending, and imports by businesses. In fact, as growth rates have returned to positive values, the trade deficit has again widened. Even if a trade surplus were to be achieved, 'net exports should be multiplied by three in a single year' (something 'highly improbable'; Gracia and Paz, 2013: 7) in order to offset the depressive effect of adjustment measures on domestic demand and growth.

As Álvarez et al. (2013: 89) state, 'European construction and the dynamics of the community economies have consolidated a productive geography crisscrossed by major fractures among countries', thus promoting 'the emergence of growing divergences between the centre and the periphery in terms of growth, inflation, and external balance, as well as the accumulation of high debt levels in some countries' (*op.cit.*: 107). In particular, although before the crisis Spain's economy gained overall importance in European industrial production, it did so in areas of low or medium technological intensity and with lower productivity, causing the trade deficit vis-á-vis the rest of the Eurozone to increase from the very beginning of the monetary integration process.

In sum, fiscal austerity and labor market reforms have been completely ineffective in achieving the objectives they purportedly pursued. On the one hand, despite tax increases and public spending cuts, public debt continued to grow (up to €1 trillion in 2014, or 100.4% of GDP, a record high). On the other hand, although fiscal and wage adjustments have depressed domestic demand and, at the same time, imports reduced the Spanish trade deficit for some years, the deficit has picked up again, going from its nadir of 1.4% of GDP in 2013 to 2.0% in 2015. Since 2007, the only component of aggregate demand that has contributed positively to growth every year has been exports. As new elections came nearer, in 2014 the public sector again adopted a more active role, and with it the other components of domestic demand: since then, investment, private consumption, and public consumption have joined exports in a positive trend. However, social conditions remain far from what they were before the crisis, and the measures adopted have ensured that the burden of the crisis has fallen on working classes by way of both the welfare state retrenchment and the labor market adjustment. Meanwhile, thanks to the socialization of financial losses and the contraction of wages, the banking sector has been successfully restructured (in terms of its interests) and profitability by companies has been partially restored.

As shown in Chapter 1, in 2010, GDP growth rates were recovering slightly, returning to slightly positive territory. Then a new round of fiscal and labor adjustments made first by the PSOE and then by the new PP government generated a relapse decline in GDP between 2011 and 2013, fostering what became a double-dip recession. Since 2013 Q3, the quarterly rates of growth have returned to positive. However, with an Industrial Production Index still far below levels prior to the crisis, this growth remains deeply insufficient to achieving a sustained recovery in employment figures, which in 2015 barely reached 2010 levels, mainly through short-term and/or part-time jobs. Figures are still well below 2007 levels, and much lower in other associated indicators such as wages. As a consequence, the adjustment process continues to have a strong negative impact on inequality, poverty, and living conditions indicators (especially for women, given the unequal share of care work, among other factors; see Vicent et al., 2013).

According to Eurostat data, during the 2007–2014 period, the share of income of the top 10% richest households increased by 2.7% annually, whereas its share of available income rose from 23.6% to 24.7%. By contrast, the income of the bottom 10% poorest households fell by 0.7% annually, whereas its share of available income dropped from 2.4% to 1.8%. Consequently, the country's Gini Index has increased from 31.9 to 34.5 points in 2016. Thus, Spain has become one of the most unequal countries in the European Union. This, together with the worsening of access to public services, has led to an increase in social exclusion and material deprivation suffered in Spanish society. The percentage of people at risk of exclusion has increased to 27.9% in 2016, from 23.3% in 2007. Severe material deprivation at the same time rose from 3.5% to 5.8%. Thus emerges a clear picture of losers and winners, as a consequence of both the economic dynamics and the economic policies implemented.

At the same time, housing, previously at the center of the wealth effect, became a luxury when the unemployed and underemployed could not meet their mortgage payments. Mortgage foreclosures increased from 25,943 in 2007 to a peak of 93,636 in 2010, and that figure in 2015 remained as high as 68,135. Although we lack official data for evictions before 2013, it is worth noting that between that year and 2015, the percentage of foreclosures that ended in evictions ranged between 31% and 43% (all data from the General Council of the Judiciary). Data from the Bank of Spain (from financial institutions) show that repossession of foreclosed dwellings reached 110,140 between 2012 and 2014 (the only period currently available). Meanwhile, management of the 'bad bank' building assets portfolio has contributed to the gradual recovery of housing prices, thus ensuring new business opportunities for the building sector.

In short, the response to the crisis took the form of a process of fiscal austerity and labor market adjustment, which has left the Spanish economy in a position of great weakness, despite the relatively high growth rates achieved after periods of GDP decline (2008–2010) and relapse (2011–2013). Although government debt has barely been contained, structural stagnation of the growth model makes it impossible to reverse the external imbalances of the economy. In the face of highly precarious and insufficient job creation, an increasingly regressive pattern of income distribution, and the retrenchment of the welfare state (with consequences to the share of care work between women and men; Alonso and Trillo, 2015), living conditions have worsened for a large majority of the population. In this way, the key actors in the buildup of the Spanish growth model during the pre-crisis period have safeguarded their positions, blocking the long-needed transformation of Spain's productive and distributive patterns. The link between all these processes will be analyzed in detail throughout the book.

Structure of the book

As previously stated, the main concern of the book is the evolution of Spain's economy, our goal being twofold: on the one hand, we provide explanation of the causes of the current crisis; on the other, we analyze the economic adjustments imposed as a reaction to that crisis and the consequences thereof, focusing on the effects on inequality, living conditions, and wages (again, taking wages in their broadest sense, as a social relationship).

Our explanation centers on five analytical axes: the evolution of the growth model; the external insertion (in terms of production and trade); the financial sector and its influence on the rest of the economy; changes in the labor market; and the distributional consequences of both the expansive phase and the subsequent crisis.

In Chapter 1, we show the main limitations of the Spanish economy's process of accumulation and, in particular the concurrent evolution of capital investment, productivity, and profitability. The formation of a housing bubble is explained as the consequence of a downward trend in the rate of profitability.

The chapter's main contributions are related to the consideration (based on Shaikh, 2016) of the growth model as the concrete form adopted by the process of capital accumulation, which we apply to the study of the Spanish case. This requires the quantitative estimation of surplus, capital stock, and profitability (as well as its components) for the whole period. Our results show the links between the downward trend of wages and the evolution of productivity, as well as the restructuring of production. In addition, the chapter completes its contribution with an input–output analysis (including its knock-on effects) to accurately determine the impact of the real estate sector in the growth dynamics and its role in the subsequent breakup of the model. Finally, environmental imbalances are also evaluated.

Chapter 2 deals with the role of Spain in the international fragmentation of production. In particular, two interrelated dimensions of the economy's international economic relationships are examined: the productive and trade spheres. The chapter assumes that the capitalist world economy is a hierarchical structure, which leads to the emergence of international economic relations of dependency and dominion. The Spanish economy is characterized as a peripheral economy after examining two aspects: i) the control foreign capital exerts on those economic sectors that are most technologically intensive and most dynamic in terms of exports; and ii) the technological dependence of the intra- and inter-industrial pattern of specialization.

This chapter links thus Chapter 1 with Chapter 3 by revealing the structural origins of the financial turmoil caused by the process of indebtedness and its bonds with the growth model. It paves the way to the explanation of the adjustment on wages based on the role of Spain in the international division of labor, which is key to understanding the difference among the current account deficit of Spain, Ireland, or the United States. Our results show the existence of a core–periphery pattern also in intra-industry trade and the limits of the crisis management strategy (internal devaluation) to modify Spain's mode of external insertion.

In Chapter 3, the crucial dynamics of indebtedness are explained in detail. The chapter begins by describing the basic components of the Spanish financial system. Next, light is shed on the system's role in financing the pre-crisis growth model. Specifically, we highlight the effects of integration into the EMU and of overindebtedness by banks, companies, and households. Finally, we address the process through which a private debt crisis became a public debt crisis and a balance sheet recession following the collapse of the housing bubble. Throughout the whole analysis, the chapter studies also the close links between the banking sector and the government as well as the role played by banking regulation.

Although the debt crisis is a worldwide phenomenon, the chapter focuses on the specific elements without which it is not possible to understand the severity of the crisis in Spain. Membership in the EMU has been an aggravating factor in the excessive use of (external) debt during the expansionary period, but also in limiting the implementation of an appropriate crisis management strategy. The chapter concludes that the crisis management started from a misdiagnosis of the situation by focusing on liquidity problems in the financial sector and neglecting solvency problems. As a consequence, not only has it been ineffective in addressing the private debt crisis, but also counterproductive as it has harmed economic activity. In addition, our analysis shows that the management strategy has been notably unfair because it has transferred a large part of the costs to the social groups that had fewer resources to face the situation.

Chapter 4 is devoted to the effects of labor market reforms aimed at increasing external competitiveness and decreasing debt (which relates to problems analyzed in Chapters 2 and 3). Our analysis is based on the structural aspects that characterize labor relations in Spain and that explain the implications of labor market deregulation in recent decades. We detail the main changes that such a market has experienced, both before and after the current crisis, as well as the consequences those changes have had for labor. We show how corporate strategies, labor market policies, and the role played by labor unions, added since the beginning of the crisis to internal devaluation policies, have weakened collective bargaining and have led to the spread of precarious employment and the impoverishment of workers.

Chapter 5 tackles the impact of the adjustment process on inequalities, thus considering the wider scope of that process. This chapter provides a comprehensive view of the distributive pattern of the economy based on the analysis of its structural causes (which are related to the analyses made in Chapters 1, 2, and 3), explaining thus the trends of increasing inequalities and poverty, both during the expansive phase and afterwards.

Our contribution here resides in the systematic breakdown of the components of the primary distribution of income (pre-distribution), that is, wealth distribution (including a class perspective, instead of a personal income perspective), functional income distribution, wage dispersion, and the sources of richest people's income, as well as the components of the secondary distribution of income, including the role of welfare state reforms since the mid-1990s. Our results determine how the combination of welfare state cutbacks and labor market reforms analyzed in Chapter 4 have led to the increase in inequality and poverty, and this affects the stratification of the Spanish society.

The order in which we present our explanation is not random. Each chapter is related to the previous, and understanding of the crisis in Spain and the consequences thereof requires the gathering together of all five elements. The first three form a 'causal triangle' inasmuch as they offer explanation of the whole process from different angles. The subsequent two are focused on analysis of the consequences of the dynamics explained in the other chapters, including the adjustments implemented in order to contain the crisis and covering both labor conditions and distributive struggles. In addition, there are some cross-section areas (the ecological question, gender issues, and the immigration problems), which serve to complement the central perspective: the division between capital and labor.

We finally close the book with a brief concluding chapter where we also offer an outlook on the foreseeable future. As we shall see, the adjustment policies imposed by the Troika and adopted by the Spanish government are merely strengthening the growth model and the trade pattern that prevailed before the crisis. As a consequence, the impacts on the labor market continue to be severely negative, magnifying the existing problems of temporariness and unemployment; and income inequality, monetary poverty, and social exclusion continue to worsen from already high levels. It may be said Spain is today suffering its own 'lost decade', as the Latin American economies did previously.

Notes

1 Author names are given in alphabetical order, as both share equal responsibility for this chapter.
2 Sanabria and Medialdea (2014) use data from the Bank of Spain, which are not strictly comparable to data used by Lapavitsas et al. (2010).

References

Alonso, N. and Trillo, D. (2015): 'La crisis del estado de bienestar y sus repercusiones sobre la situación sociolaboral de las mujeres', *Revista de Economía Crítica*, 20, pp. 135–154.
Álvarez, N., Buendía, L., Mateo, J.P., Medialdea, B., Molero, R., Montanyà, M., Paz, M.J. and Sanabria, A. (2008): 'La relación salarial en Estados Unidos y Latinoamérica bajo las políticas neoliberales', *Razón y Revolución*, 18, pp. 189–205.
———. (2009): *Ajuste y salario: Las consecuencias del neoliberalismo en América Latina y Estados Unidos*, Madrid: Fondo de Cultura Económica.
———. (2011): 'La naturaleza salarial del ajuste estructural en América Latina y Estados Unidos', in J.P. Mateo, R. Molero and R. Santana (comps.), *Globalización, dependencia y crisis económica: Análisis heterodoxos desde la economía del desarrollo*, Málaga: FIM-CEDMA, pp. 108–132.
Álvarez, I., Luengo, F. and Uxó, J. (2013): *Fracturas y crisis en Europa*, Madrid: Clave Intelectual.
Aragón, J., Martínez, A., Cruces, J. and Rocha, F. (2010): 'La integración laboral de las personas inmigrantes en España: Una aproximación al empleo y las condiciones de trabajo aguilera', *Informes de la Fundación 1 de Mayo*, 2010–20, Madrid.
Bank of Spain (2016): 'Nota informativa sobre ayudas públicas en el proceso de reestructuración del sistema bancario español (2009–2016)'. Available at: www.bde.es/f/webbde/GAP/Secciones/SalaPrensa/NotasInformativas/Briefing_notes/es/notabe060916.pdf (Last Access: 02/16/2017).

Banyuls, J. and Recio, A. (2015): 'Crisis dentro de la crisis: España bajo el neoliberalismo conservador', in L. Steffen (ed.), *El triunfo de las ideas fracasadas. Modelos de capitalismo europeo en la crisis*, Madrid: La Catarata, pp. 39–69.

Boyer, R. (2012): 'The Four Fallacies of Contemporary Austerity Policies: The Lost Keynesian Legacy', *Cambridge Journal of Economics*, 36 (1), pp. 283–312.

Buendía, L. (2013): '¿Quién paga la factura: regresión salarial y desigualdad', in V. Alonso (coord.), *¿Lo llamaban democracia? De la crisis económica al cuestionamiento de un régimen político*, Barcelona: Icaria, pp. 37–43. Available at: www.icariaeditorial.com/pdf_libros/lo%20llamaban%20democracia%20tripa.pdf (Last Access: 02/16/2017).

Callinicos, A. (2012): 'Contradictions of Austerity', *Cambridge Journal of Economics*, 36 (1), pp. 65–77.

Carpintero, O. (2005): *El metabolismo de la economía española: Recursos naturales y huella ecológica (1955–2000)*, Lanzarote: Fundación César Manrique.

Consejo Económico y Social (CES) (2012): *La internacionalización de la empresa española como factor de competitividad*, Madrid: CES.

Duménil, G. and Lévy, D. (2011): *The Crisis of Neoliberalism*, Cambridge, MA: Harvard University Press.

Edwards, S. (1995): *Crisis and Reform in Latin America: From Despair to Hope*, Washington, DC: World Bank/Oxford University Press.

Fernández-Villaverde, J. and Ohanian, L. (2010): 'The Spanish Crisis from a Global Perspective', *Documentos de trabajo* (FEDEA), 3, Madrid.

Fundación Banco Bilbao Vizcaya Argentaria (FBBVA) (2014): 'El stock y los servicios del capital en España y su distribución territorial y sectorial (1964–2012)', *Documentos de trabajo (Fundación BBVA)*, 1. Available at: www.fbbva.es/TLFU/microsites/stock09/fbbva_stock08_index.html (Last Access: 02/16/2017).

Garzón, A. (2013): 'El capitalismo español en el siglo XXI: ¿Qué lugar en la economía mundial', *Pensar desde abajo*, 2, pp. 11–39.

Gereffi, G. and Korzeniewick, R.P. (1994): *Commodity Chains and Global Capitalism*, Westport: Praeger.

Gouverneur, J. (1983): *Contemporary Capitalism and Marxist Economics*, Totowa, NJ: Rowman & Littlefield.

Gracia, M. and Paz, M.J. (2013): '¿La política de devaluación interna puede reducir el déficit exterior de nuestra economía y sus necesidades de financiación externa?', *Economía a debate*, Fundación 1 de Mayo. Available at: www.1mayo.ccoo.es/nova/files/1018/F1MMariaJosePaz.pdf (Last Access: 02/16/2017).

Greer, S. (2014): 'Structural Adjustment Comes to Europe: Lessons for the Eurozone From the Conditionality Debates', *Global Social Policy*, 14 (1), pp. 51–71.

Harcourt, G. (1999): ' "Horses for Courses": The Making of a Post-Keynesian Economist', in A. Heertje (ed.), *The Makers of Modern Economics*, Volume IV, Cheltenham, UK and Northampton, MA: Edward Elgar Publishing, pp. 32–69.

Harvey, D. (2005): *A Brief History of Neoliberalism*, New York: Oxford University Press.

Hermann, C. (2016): 'Another "Lost Decade"? Crisis and Structural Adjustment in Europe and Latin America', *Globalizations*, first published on-line, 10/05/2016.

Hopkins, T. and Wallerstein, I. (1977): 'Patterns of Development of the Modern World-System', *Review (Fernand Brudel Center)*, 1 (2), pp. 111–145.

Howard, M. and King, J. (2008): *The Rise of Neoliberalism in Advanced Capitalist Economies: A Materialist Analysis*, London: Palgrave Macmillan.

International Monetary Fund (IMF) (2009): 'Spain: Selected Issues', *IMF Country Report* No. 09/129, Washington: IMF.

Kalecki, M. (1943): 'Political Aspects of Full Employment', *The Political Quarterly*, 14, pp. 322–330.

Keen, S. (2011): *Debunking Economics: The Neaked Emperor Dethroned*, Revised and Expanded Edition. London: Zed Books.

Lapavitsas, C., Kaltenbrunner, A., Lambrinidis, G., Lindo, D., Meadway, J., Michell, J., Painceira, J.P., Pires, E., Powell, J., Stenfors, A. and Teles, N. (2010): *The Eurozone Between Austerity and Default*, London: Research on Money and Finance.

López, I. and Rodríguez, E. (2010): *Fin de ciclo. Financiarización, territorio y sociedad de propietarios en la onda larga del capitalismo hispano (1959–2010)*, Madrid: Traficantes de Sueños.

———. (2011a): 'Del auge al colapso. El modelo financiero-inmobiliario', *Revista de Economía Crítica*, 12, pp. 39–63.

———. (2011b): 'The Spanish Model', *New Left Review*, 69, pp. 5–28.

Mandel, E. (1967): *An Introduction to Marxist Economic Theory*, Chippendale: Resistance Books, 2002.

Mateo, J.P. and Montanyà, M. (2014): 'Acumulación de capital y burbuja inmobiliaria en España', paper presented to XIV Jornadas de Economía Crítica, Valladolid (Spain). Available at: http://pendientedemigracion.ucm.es/info/ec/jec14/comunica/A_EM/A_EM_11.pdf (Last Access: 02/16/2017).

Minsky, H. (1992): 'The Financial Instability Hypothesis', *Working Paper (Levy Economics Institute)*, 74 (May).

Molero, R. (2014): 'La desigualdad de la renta en el modelo de crecimiento de la economía española. Alternativas a las políticas de ajuste', *Estudios de Progreso 82/2014*, Madrid: Fundación Alternativas. Available at: www.fundacionalternativas.org/public/storage/estudios_documentos_archivos/98aaa551bf4a0497300ea68ed26504e8.pdf (Last Access: 02/16/2017).

Moreno, L. (2012): *La Europa asocial. Crisis y estado de bienestar*, Barcelona: Península.

Muñoz de Bustillo, R. and Antón, J.I. (2014): 'Turning Back Before Arriving: The Dismantling of the Spanish Welfare State', in D. Vaughan-Whitehead (ed.), *Dismantling the European Social Model: Europe Losing Its Soul*, Cheltenham: Edward Elgar, pp. 341–381.

Murillo, F.J. (2010): 'Impacto salarial del milagro económico español', *Análisis Económico*, XXV (59), pp. 179–204.

Navarro, V. (2006): *El subdesarrollo social de España*, Anagrama: Barcelona.

Palley, T. (2013), 'Europe's Crisis Without End: The Consequences of Neoliberalism', *Contributions to Political Economy*, 32 (1), pp. 29–50.

Pérez, S. (1999): 'From Labor to Finance Understanding the Failure of Socialist Economic Policies in Spain', *Comparative Political Studies*, 32 (6), pp. 659–689.

Prebisch, R. (1962): 'El desarrollo económico de la América Latina y algunos de sus principales problemas', *Boletín económico de América Latina*, 7 (1).

Recio, A. and Banyuls, J. (2004): '¿Crecimiento del empleo sin tecnología? La paradoja del mercado de trabajo en España', paper presented to IX Jornadas de Economía Crítica, Madrid (Spain).

Recio, A., de Alós-Moner, R. and Olivares, I. (2006): 'Construction in Spain. Towards a new Regulation?', *QUIT Working Paper*, 13. Available at: http://quit.uab.es (Last Access: 02/16/2017).

Rodríguez Cabrero, G. (2011): 'The Consolidation of the Spanish Welfare State (1975–2010)', in A.M. Guillén and M. León (eds.), *The Spanish Welfare State in European Context*, Surrey: Ashgate Publishing.

Ruiz-Gálvez, M.E. (2015): 'La realidad salarial de los jóvenes en España desde una per-spectiva comparada', *ICEI Working Papers: Desempleo Juvenil en España*, 2. Available at: www.ucm.es/data/cont/docs/430-2016-01-22-Volumen2%20definitivo.pdf (Last Access: 02/16/2017).

Sanabria, A. (2009) 'La naturaleza salarial del ajuste', in N. Álvarez, L. Buendía, J.P. Mateo, B. Medialdea, R. Molero, M. Montanyà, M.J. Paz and A. Sanabria (eds.), *Ajuste y salario. Las consecuencias del neoliberalismo en América Latina y Estados Unidos*, Madrid: Fondo de Cultura Económica.

Sanabria, A. and Garzón, E. (2013): 'El "rescate" bancario español: un "botín" multimil-lonario', *Viento Sur*, 131, pp. 101–112. Available at: http://vientosur.info/IMG/pdf/VS131_A_Sanabria_E_Garzon_Rescate_bancario_espan_ol-botin.pdf (Last Access: 02/16/2017).

Sanabria, A. and Medialdea, B. (2014): 'La crisis de la deuda en España: elementos básicos y alternativas', in FOESSA (ed.), *Análisis y perspectivas 2014: Precariedad y Cohesión Social*, Madrid: FOESSA, pp. 63–70.

———. (2016): 'Lending Calling. Recession by Over-Indebtedness: Description and Spe-cific Features of the Spanish Case', *Panoeconomicus*, 63 (2) (special issue), pp. 195–210.

Seminari Taifa (2010): 'La crisis en el Estado español: el rescate de los poderosos', *Informes de economía crítica*, 7. Available at: http://informes.seminaritaifa.org/files/2010/06/Informe_07_ES.pdf (Last Access: 02/16/2017).

Shaikh, A. (1980): 'The Laws of International Exchange', in E.J. Nell (ed.), *Growth, Prof-its and Property: Essays in the Revival of Political Economy*, Cambridge (UK): Cam-bridge University Press, pp. 204–235.

———. (2016): *Capitalism: Competition, Conflict, Crises*, New York: Oxford University Press.

Vasapollo, L. (2012): *Crisis of Capitalism: Compendium of Applied Economics*, Boston: Brill.

Vicent, L., Castro, C., Agenjo, A., and Herrero, Y. (2013): *El desigual impacto de la cri-sis sobre las mujeres*, Madrid: FUHEM. Available at: www.fuhem.es/media/cdv/file/biblioteca/Dossier/dossier_El-desigual-impacto-de-la-crisis-sobre-las-mujeres.pdf (Last Access: 02/16/2017).

Zack, G., Poncela, P., Senra, E. and Sotelsek, D. (2013): 'Towards an Effective Structural Budget Balance for Economic Stability', *Documentos de Trabajo UC-CIFF-IELAT*, 13.

1 The accumulation model of the Spanish economy

Profitability, the real estate bubble, and sectoral imbalances

Juan Pablo Mateo and Miguel Montanyà Revuelto[1]

Introduction

Our analysis begins with an explanation of the basic characteristics of the growth model of the Spanish economy. In particular, this first chapter addresses the dynamics followed by the process of capital accumulation in Spain during the period 1995–2015. The study of the economic performance requires consideration of both the fundamental features of the growth period (up to 2007–2008) and the specific aspects of the economic crisis that led to a long recession, still in effect today.[2] The two phenomena are interrelated, and investigation of the economic boom provides the keys to the subsequent crisis.

Theoretically, we commence with a political economy approach because the generation of surplus is considered the preeminent object of production. Therefore, the level of capital valorization, as reflected in the rate of profit, ultimately governs the process of capital accumulation and, consequently, cycles of expansion and crisis. However, the process of economic reproduction is inherently turbulent (Shaikh, 2016), subject to various contradictions, and takes different forms depending on the type of economy and its historical context.

In this sense, it is necessary to refer to the integration of Spain into the Economic and Monetary Union (EMU), the vital element of which (from the political economy perspective) is the formation of a space for valorization endowed with a common currency for heterogeneous economic structures in terms of productive development. Since 1997, a fixed nominal parity for Spain's erstwhile national currency, the peseta, was established, and monetary integration took place in 1999, although the euro did not begin to physically circulate until January 1, 2002. The particularities of the Spanish economy were not independent of this integration. As we shall see in Chapter 2, the Spanish economy developed a dependent manner of insertion, both in terms of European integration and into the global economy. The country's levels of mechanization and productivity have historically been lower than in more central economies, featuring specialization in branches with lower capital stock per worker, thus taking advantage of the lower costs of labor.

The peripheral nature of the Spanish economy within the European Union (EU) has had several implications, which will be addressed throughout this book. As we shall see in Chapter 2, the pattern of Spanish trade has long shown a tendency to generate deficits, as well as a persistent dependence on foreign capital in branches with greater technological intensity, a trend that became worse since Spain entered the common market. Chapter 3 shows that, because of Spain's membership in the euro, the conditions for borrowing became more favorable; but with the outbreak of the crisis, finances were instrumental in fomenting an extraordinarily regressive restructuring process. Chapter 4 explains that high unemployment has been a peculiar feature of the Spanish economy since the crisis of the 1970s, allowing wage dynamics to be regulated, partly due to the influence of EU institutions, depending on the needs of capital accumulation, in contrast to the repressive mechanisms in force during the period of the dictatorship. In addition, Spain has suffered from underdevelopment of its welfare state, because its consolidation coincided partially with the neoliberal restructuring of the 1980s, aggravated later by the Growth and Stability Pact, as explained in Chapter 5. The victory of the Socialist Party in 1982 led, paradoxically, to a period of retreat for the labor movement, which has contributed to a progressive precariousness of labor and a worsening of the distribution of wealth and income in what has been historically one of the more unequal countries in Europe.

Given the integration of Spain into the EMU, the theoretical starting point for this chapter is the concept of the development of productive forces, an idea with a qualitative (structural) as well as a quantitative dimension. This development is reflected first in surplus production capacity, expressed in the profitability of capital, and second in indicators such as the degrees of mechanization of the productive process, productivity, and costs (competitiveness), along with the sectoral articulation, which in turn has determined the character of external insertion. Thus, the foundation of investment (I) is the rate of profit (r), which measures the amount of profit (p) per unit of capital (K), $r = p/K$.[3] The growth of output (Q) depends on the investment, materialized in the stock of capital (K), in turn driven by the rate of profit. The profitability of capital can be related to several heterogeneous factors related to value added (VA), production technology, and the sphere of distribution:

$$r = \frac{VA - W}{K} = \left(\frac{q - w}{\theta} \right) P_{yk}$$

In capitalism, technical change takes the form of a tendency toward an increase in the quantity of means of production (mp) per unit of labor (L), which can be approached, even if imperfectly, with the K/L ratio, $K/L = \Theta$. This capital–labor ratio constitutes the mechanism to reduce costs by generating a margin of productivity (q) with respect to the real wage per worker (w), so that Θ ultimately determines the evolution of productivity. To the extent that the achieved increase in output is lower than the increase in the quantity of capital stock required (i.e., productivity improvement is less than the increase in the capital–labor ratio, as may be expected as a tendency), the capital–output ratio (K/Q) (inverse of the product–capital ratio, or the 'labor productivity of capital') will be increased, meaning that the maximum rate of profit (r_{max}) will decrease, considering that price indices evolve in a balanced way ($P_{yk} = P_y/P_k$ around unity):

$$r_{max} = \frac{VA}{K} = \frac{q}{\theta} \Leftrightarrow P_{yk} \to 1$$

Thus, the rate of profit depends positively on whether a given technical change can improve productivity, containing wages and relatively cheapening the capital stock assets.

However, the rate of capital accumulation depends instead on the differential of profitability in relation to the cost of financing (interest rates, i), or net profitability ($r - i$) (Shaikh, 2016). But because the level of 'i' depends on the total capacity to generate surplus, it is not independent of gross profitability.[4] Therefore, the role of finance is conditioned by the level of productive development, and in particular by the process of capital valorization.

In the case of the Spanish economy, the process of capital accumulation since the late 1990s, and to a greater extent since 2002, has been driven by the revaluation of construction-related assets, especially residential assets. It can thus be characterized as real estate financial capitalism based on asset inflation (Rodríguez and López, 2010). To carry out a political economy analysis, it is necessary to provide the material basis for explaining the massive reorientation of capital towards these activities in opposition to other explanatory proposals based on agents' preferences and their utility schemes. The construction sector has multiple direct and indirect connections with other non-financial activities: building materials, machinery, etc. (Cuadrado-Roura, 2010); and it requires a set of corollary services such as sewage, electricity, and water systems, as well as sanitary, educational, and cultural services, along with commercial and transport infrastructures. Thus, this activity is able to drive a process of accumulation and to configure (or restructure) a given economic structure. The axis of this accumulation model in Spain has had profound implications on the distribution of income, the financial sector, and sectoral and productive imbalances, as we will see throughout the book.

Nonetheless, the relevant dimension of housing is that, along with its character as a consumer good, it is an asset that can be bought and resold for profit. Its production requires a relatively long time frame, during which increases in the price of housing will raise profitability and attract more capital. In the short term, this price (which includes the land rent) can be determined by demand, because supply is relatively inelastic and takes some years to respond. Compared with the production of other goods, real estate prices may increase because the expectation of price rises leads to the property becoming not a consumer good, but an asset or means of valorization. Therefore, residential activity can form an alternative (secondary) circuit for the relatively autonomous investment of the primary sphere of value generation (Gotham, 2006).

In this chapter, we analyze the implications that these factors have had for Spain's economic growth model. Specifically, the next section addresses the dynamics of capital accumulation during the most recent boom period and their implications in terms of aggregate demand. In the third section we explain how this process was truncated by a series of imbalances immanent to the process of accumulation, aggravated by sectoral imbalances (especially the aforementioned real estate bubble), all of which had significant implications for the evolution of demand and its economic relation with the environment. In the end, we conclude that all these imbalances have made the dynamics of accumulation unsustainable, until it broke down with the emergence of the crisis.

Macroeconomic dynamics: from growth to long depression

General aspects of the Spanish economy

In relation to the EU, the Spanish economic structure has featured greater participation by agrarian activities and by services oriented towards the hotel industry and commerce (due to the importance of tourism), with a lesser development of business services. In terms of industry, Spain maintains a relative specialization in manufactures of low and medium technological content, whereas the construction sector has played a central role in the process of accumulation (García and Myro, 2015).

In 1995, Spain's GDP per employee accounted for 74% of the Eurozone-12 average, and since then that figure has grown by just over a third (36%) of the relative increase throughout the zone (AMECO, 2017). However, overall GDP growth averaged 3.8% per year in 1995–2007, and 3.6% to 2008, when GDP growth began to slow. In other words, Spain enjoyed one of the most intense growth rates of all the developed economies, whereas the EU-28, the Eurozone, and the OECD group averaged levels below 3% per annum (AMECO, 2017; OECD, 2017). In per capita terms, however, Spain's average was lower, at 2.6%, closer to the level registered in the more advanced areas (at 2% to 2.2% per annum) (OECD, 2017). In the second quarter of 2008, Spain's GDP stagnated, and in the following quarter it fell by 0.8% with respect to the previous quarter, commencing a sustained path of setbacks that in the fourth quarter of 2008 became absolute declines in year-on-year terms (INE, 2016b). In 2015, GDP at current prices was still 3.6% lower than that of 2008's peak (INE, 2016a), indicating the serious depth of the Great Recession.

During the last expansionary cycle, the component that carried quantitatively more weight in the GDP was household consumption, although its relative participation diminished by four percentage points (Table 1.1). However, investment was the real engine in the boom. Economic expansion was characterized by an intense increase in gross fixed capital formation (GFCF), reaching 6.4% per year until 2007. This was higher than increases in private consumption, public spending, and exports, although imports rose by even more (at 8.6% per annum) due to the economic boom and, in particular, domestic demand. As a result, GFCF went from representing 22% of GDP in 1995–1997 to 31% in 2006–2007.

During the post-2008 crisis period, investment has remained at substantially lower levels. In 2013–2014, it failed to exceed 20% of GDP, falling by 6% per

Table 1.1 GDP and its components (aggregate demand), 1995–2016

Demand and total output	Structure (%)				Average rates of change	
	1995	*2000*	*2007*	*2015*	*1995–2007*	*2008–2016*
CONS	60.95	59.70	56.98	58.11	3.61	−1.20
GOV	17.65	16.73	17.68	19.38	4.26	−0.01
GFCF	22.02	26.14	31.05	19.72	6.37	−4.69
X	21.93	28.62	25.71	33.18	6.49	2.70
M	22.90	31.62	31.70	30.73	8.66	−1.37
GDP	100.00	100.00	100.00	100.00	3.78	−0.68
VA	72.99	73.32	69.47	66.04	3.41	−1.02

Note: CONS: consumption; GOV: government expenditures; GFCF: gross fixed capital formation; X: exports; M: imports; GDP: gross domestic product; VA: value added in productive activities. Structure (current prices) and average rates of change (constant prices).

year. Taking into account that depreciation increased from 13% in the second half of the 1990s to 15% in 2006–2008 and surpassed 17% from 2011 (OECD, 2017), the increase in production capacity (net investment) has been minimal during the recessive phase. As shown in Figure 1.1, if in the first phase of the crisis public spending increased as a consequence of demand stimulus policies, once these were suspended in 2010 due to increased debt, this component of demand only worsened the GDP. Thus, between 2010 and 2013, only exports could partially halt the contraction in output.

In short, investment has played a central role in the macroeconomic dynamics of the Spanish economy. The following section addresses its essential foundation (the profitability of capital) in order to analyze the dynamics of accumulation and to further understand the crisis.

Production of surplus

The impulse toward accumulation can be explained by the rate of corporate profit. However, the existence of a real estate bubble implies that profitability has also been linked to the revaluation of certain assets, a reality not captured in the National Accounts. Therefore, this section offers various expressions of profitability and argues that the crisis that erupted in 2008 originated in the insufficient generation of surplus, whose difficulties began to manifest two years earlier.

As seen in Figure 1.2, the mass of total surplus at constant prices peaked in 2006. In the second half of the 1990s, it had grown at 2.8% per annum, but after 2000 that pace slowed, to an expansion around half of that rate (1.5%). Between 2006 and 2013, the mass of profits fell by 11.5%, revealing the extent of the crisis of valorization. The rate of profit fell over 40% until 2012–2015 (the minimum was reached in 2013), most intensely after 2000, when it fell by more than 3% per annum. By 2007, the decline had reached 26.5%, and in seven years during the crisis it fell by another 20%. In relation to the conventional index of profitability for non-financial corporations, a different evolution can be perceived. The

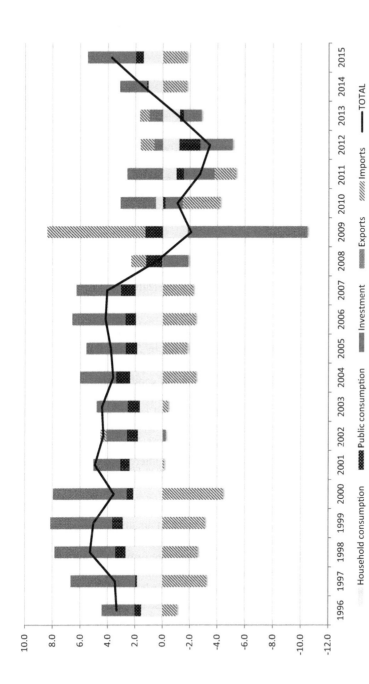

Figure 1.1 Quantitative contribution to GDP growth of demand variables, 1995–2015 (%)

Source: Own elaboration with data from INE.

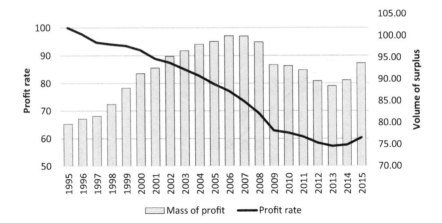

Figure 1.2 Profit rate (%) and volume of surplus at constant prices (1995 = 100), 1995–2015

Notes: Profit rate: gross operating surplus of productive activities, net non-residential capital stock (year t-1). Mass of surplus deflated by the capital stock price index.

Source: Own elaboration with data from FBBVA (2017) and INE (2016a).

ordinary return on net assets remained constant until 2002, but then it fell by 40% from 2006 to 2015, whereas the return on equity fell by 53% in 2006–2014 (Bank of Spain, BoS, 2017d).

One of the factors that has shaped the dynamics of capital valorization has been the cost of financing. On the one hand, interest rates declined relatively more than profitability. The long-term interest rate in real terms (excluding the GDP deflator) stood at 6.3% in 1995, but in 2000–2001 it was under 1%. Afterward, it reached negative levels between 2003 and 2006, bottoming in 2005 at −0.95%, but recovering in 2007, when it reached 1%. These interest rates rose to 3.9% in 2008, and by 2011–2012 they exceeded 5%, subsequently falling to 2.7% in 2014 and to 1.7% in 2015 (OECD, 2017).

The reduction in the cost of financing made it possible to overcome the inability of the Spanish economy to generate surplus value in an amount sufficient for the valorization of capital. By strongly limiting the lower level (interest rates), it was possible to compensate for the fall in the higher rate (gross profitability); but at the same time this favored the creation of a bubble in the price of assets linked to construction. The spread of return on investment minus the cost debt created a very volatile dynamic, first with a spectacular increase until the years 2004–2007, although even in 1995 this had become negative. From the peak of 2006, the fall reached an outstanding 66% until the minimum of 2012, albeit with a weak recovery in the following years. Thus, the interest rate hike was not the cause of the crisis, but it served as a functional mechanism for corporate restructuring (see Mateo, 2017), increasing the interest burden for non-financial corporations, which went from 13% in 2004–2005 to 20% to 26% in 2008–2014. Indeed, this further reduced the net profitability of small businesses, which spent more than 30% of their income on interest payments between 2008 and 2012 (BoS, 2017d).

Indebted in order to buy, with the goal of selling higher

As explained, the essential aspect of the formation and long-term maintenance of the housing bubble was the underlying problem of capital valorization in Spain. Moreover, this occurred in a context characterized by high quantities of capital in search of profitability, largely stemming from current account surpluses in the more advanced economies of the Eurozone, which sought to obtain attractive valorization in a context of reduced interest rates (Fernández and García, 2016).

In the case of Spain, integration into an area of higher productive development meant a more-than-proportional cheapening of the cost of financing, which certainly favored indebtedness as a means to acquire housing as an investment asset. Consequently, housing prices departed from the objective foundation established by the law of value. Moreover, this incidence was even higher given certain peculiarities of the Spanish economy: propitious topographical and climatic conditions (mountains, beaches, sunshine) and an historical legacy in which expansive stages had long been complemented by speculative dynamics in construction, accompanied by an enabling legislative framework. The 1998 Land Law allowed for the extension of land development, marrying tax relief with the need to launder black money under the adoption of the euro; also, decentralization gave municipalities a leading role as competing urban developers (Harvey, 1973; Rodríguez and López, 2010).[5] In turn, speculative urban expansion was accompanied by a policy of investment in infrastructure that, far from being based on forecast transportation needs, prioritized large investment projects whose profitability was ensured by the public sector.[6] Consequently, Spain became an area of international valorization that served the European division of labor.

If in 1996 the price of a square meter of housing increased by only 1.4% with respect to the previous year, in the years that followed, annual growth accelerated, already reaching 7.6% by 1999. The phase with the highest increases in housing prices was 2002–2006, with an average 14.8% annual increase. Overall, the price of housing increased at an annual average of 12.4% between 1999 and 2007, the period of the real estate bubble. From 1998 these increases were higher than the mortgage rate, so the expectation of a continued rise was the justification for borrowing with the intent to resell later, especially when alternatives such as investment funds paid much lower returns (Table 1.2). In fact, investment funds in money market assets (money funds or FIAMMs), together with capital markets assets (fixed income real estate investment funds, FIMs), have yielded substantially lower returns since 1999 than those offered by revaluation of residential assets.

Therefore, the real estate bubble implied both a temporary deferral and a geographical displacement of the valorization circuit, allowing us to speak of a spatial solution, closely linked to finance, of the contradictions deriving from the production of value (valorization). The activity of construction provided a spatial

Table 1.2 Comparative evolution of price indices and investment yields in fixed income based on the mortgage interest rates for households, 1998–2007 (%)

Year	Prices indices		Interest rate	Yields	
	GDP	Housing		FIAMM	FIM
1998	2.53	5.80	5.74	3.63	12.13
1999	2.66	7.66	4.78	2.60	5.13
2000	3.28	8.58	5.79	2.01	6.76
2001	4.08	9.86	5.84	3.41	−5.32
2002	4.12	15.73	4.85	2.81	−4.23
2003	3.92	17.62	3.75	2.05	0.23
2004	3.92	17.45	3.41	1.25	4.97
2005	4.15	13.91	3.37	1.20	5.52
2006	3.98	10.41	4.23	1.48	5.73
2007	3.33	5.76	5.25	1.90	5.33

Note: Annual rate of change of GDP price deflator and average square meter of housing prices; mortgage interest rates for households; FIAMM: money market funds; FIM: capital market funds.

Source: Own elaboration with data from INE (2016a), BoS (2017c), MPW (2017).

solution to the problems of accumulation, which extended the boom at the cost of deepening the crisis and with serious environmental consequences, as we will see later.

In turn, this process has several macroeconomic implications. On the one hand, in terms of profitability, to the extent that it supposed what we can call a 'price effect', being a valuation not sustained by the extraction of surplus labor but in the form of 'capital gains' derived from changes in relative prices (Shaikh, 2016) (in this case the revaluation of assets). In this sense, this is a return that can be denominated 'fictitious' and that manifests itself as an increase in debt, which reflects the underlying fall in profitability. This further implies the need for a transfer of income between two circuits, from households (or applicants for housing) to the sphere of capital. Consequently, on the one hand, the phenomenon of debt operates as a mechanism to force such transfers of income, thus linking the financial sphere with the pattern of income distribution. On the other hand, the price effect temporarily hides the underlying problems of profitability that correspond to the value sphere.

In this sense, the price effect weighs on other activities, because it increases the cost of location for other capital goods (offices, industrial buildings, etc.) (Bellod, 2007), and this implies a redistribution of surplus to the benefit of capital invested in the sector (landowners, promoters, builders, etc.). This restructuring is not alien to the structure of the accumulation process, production costs, or competitiveness, because it has already conditioned investment flows.

Investment and capital

The period of growth was characterized by an intense rate of capital accumulation. Non-residential gross investment at constant prices in the productive area grew at 6.3% per annum between 1995 and 2007, and its subsequent fall amounted to −4.3% per year until 2013. As a result, the net non-residential productive capital (K) accumulation rate grew at an annual high of 4.6% in 1995–2007 but at only 1.4% in 2008–2015.[7]

This increase in stock was derived from investment flows that were biased toward construction assets that were mainly residential in type (Table 1.3). These investments accounted for two-thirds of the total in the initial year, and in 2007 they were almost 68%, with a relatively higher increase in housing (which in the latter year accounted for 37.8% of total stock at current prices). However, in terms of volume, investment in machinery and equipment assets saw a higher increase, above 6.5% per year, given the inflationary nature of construction assets. As a result, the volume of productive capital stock increased 70% (13 points more than the capital stock of the overall economy).

During the long depression, the accumulation process stagnated, with an annual capital stock increase of only 1.4% together with a drop in the utilization of installed capacity. Gross investment at current prices in construction assets fell from two-thirds to 50%, and its volume reached an average of −8% and −10% per year up to 2014, compared to a 2.5% to 2.7% drop for machinery and equipment.

Despite this high rate of capital accumulation, the capital–wage labor ratio remained stagnated in the 12-year-long economic boom due to the increase in the degree of salarization, having fallen by 5.2% in 2000 and partially recovering in 2007. However, the total capital–labor ratio increased by 12% in 1995–2007, or at an average of 1% per year, in any case with significant weakness (Figure 1.3). This particular evolution of the mechanization of the productive process led not only to a slow progression of labor productivity, but also to an alarming decline during the expansionary phase, which must be clarified.

The value added per full-time employee increased by 3.7% between 1995 and 2007 (or 4.6% if we take GDP, which includes net taxes on products), amounting

Table 1.3 Investment flows and capital stock, 1995–2015

Gross fixed capital formation, current prices	Structure (%)			Annual rates of change	
	1995	*2007*	*2014*	*1995–2007*	*2008–2014*
Total assets	100	100	100	6.4	−6.0
Residential	27.5	37.8	22.4	7.8	−10.1
Other constructions	37.5	30.1	29.0	4.1	−8.0
Transport equipment	7.7	7.9	9.9	8.5	−2.7
Machinery, eq. and other assets	20.1	16.5	22.8	6.7	−2.6

Net capital stock, 2010 constant prices	Total variation			
	1995–2007	*2008–2015*	*1995–2007*	*2008–2015*
Total	57.6	9.9	3.9	1.4
Non-residential	66.6	11.9	4.3	1.6
Productive	70.6	10.5	4.6	1.4

Source: Own elaboration with data from FBBVA (2017).

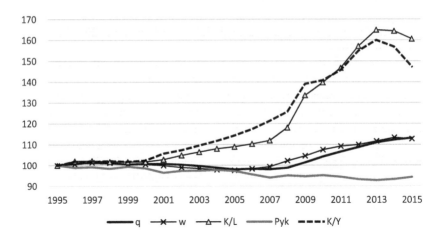

Figure 1.3 Dynamics of the components of profitability (1995 = 100), 1995–2015

Note: Productivity (q), real wage per worker (w), capital–labor ratio (K/L), relative prices (Py/Pk), capital–output ratio (K/Y).

Source: Own elaboration with data from FBBVA (2017) and INE (2016a).

to an annual average rate of 0.3%. However, the same productivity indicator, when limited only to the productive area, fell by 1.9% in that same period, or by 2.9% in terms of total hours. This is explained by the type of economic growth experienced, in which financial activities performed very favorably in terms of 'apparent productivity'; but this was a consequence of the boost to the banking and real estate sectors linked to the speculative spiral in construction. Moreover, the product generated by salaried workers, discounting the mixed income of the self-employed, fell by 5.4%.

In addition, this accumulation model driven by the revaluation of construction assets generated upward pressure on inflation. The price deflator of the productive sphere increased by an average 3.2% per year during the boom period, despite which the stock of capital price index grew even more. The P_Y/P_K ratio fell by 4.6% between 2000 and 2007, after a slight increase of 1.4% in the second half of the 1990s. Thus, in the period of fixed parity (under the euro), the assets of capital stock were raised in relation to the general price index, reflecting an underlying problem of productivity in the means of production sector, either due to production itself or due to the need to import such capital assets at higher prices. The consequences were important for the dynamics of accumulation, because on the one hand this contributes to depressing the product–capital ratio (i.e., the maximum rate of profit), which is negatively affected by the relative fall in labor productivity in relation to the capital–labor ratio. On the other hand, it intensifies the need to generate more surplus for continuation of the investment, because, in relation to the accumulation rate, the surplus value loses purchasing power.[8]

Furthermore, to the extent that inflation in Spain was higher than the Euro-zone average, the real exchange rate appreciated. The GDP deflator grew at a rate of 3.5% until 2007, whereas in the Eurozone countries it increased to 1.8% to 1.9%, depending on the number considered, so that the total percentage increase in those 12 years was 50% in Spain (twice as much as in the overall EMU). Note that the largest relative increase in GDP per worker in Spain at current prices indicated a valorization denominated in a currency whose fixed parity was not altered, although it lost purchasing power in Spain. Hence the international dimension of the real estate bubble in Spain becomes even clearer (Fernández and García, 2016).

As a result of the crisis, the pattern of the accumulation process has radically altered. One essential aspect is the profound destruction of employment. Between 2007 and 2013, total full-time employment fell by 18%, and up to 22% in the productive sphere, so the unemployment rate rose from 7.9% in the mid-2007 to 25% to 26% from the end of 2012 to the beginning of 2014 (BoS, 2017b). This job destruction, coupled with a sectoral restructuring and a fall in the use of installed capacity (by about 10 percentage points, according to BoS, 2017a), explains the contradictory recovery of the capital–labor ratio during the crisis, to more than 40% until 2013–2015, with a consequent increase in labor productivity of 15% in 2007–2015. Although the capital stock price index ceased to rise accordingly (the price ratio remaining practically constant, with a slight fall through 2013, but with a rise in the next two years, meaning a relative cheapening of the capital stock), the capital–output ratio rose until 2013 to 4.7% per year, that is, almost three times as fast as during the boom, representing an increase of 31.9% in 2007–2013, but followed by a fall in the next two years.

Characterization of the crisis

The crisis of the Spanish economy that erupted in 2008 is ultimately explained by the valorization process. As a capitalist crisis, it resulted from an inability to generate surplus in amounts sufficient to meet the needs of accumulated capital, although its external manifestation incorporated a set of peculiarities resulting from the type of capital accumulation seen in the previous period (for a discussion, see Mateo, 2017). As profitability was linked to the real estate bubble, a duality arose between the dynamics of the gross profit rate, which fell steadily throughout the period, and net profitability indicators, which began to fall only afterwards, as mentioned earlier. That is, despite the underlying fall in the gross profit rate, during the expansion phase, business expectations were high, which explains the investment boom, as has been mentioned.

Therefore, it is appropriate to analyze the evolution of the main variables on the demand side in quarterly terms (Table 1.4).[9] Gross residential investment reached a peak in 2006-Q4, and although it fell in 2007-Q1, in the following quarter it recovered partially, at which point investment in 'other buildings and constructions' stopped growing (as did total investment in construction). However, the upward phase of investment in capital goods continued until mid-2008;

Table 1.4 Quarterly evolution of GDP (demand) and housing prices, 2006–2008 (%)

Variables	2006	2007				2008			
	Q4	Q1	Q2	Q3	Q4	Q1	Q2	Q3	Q4
GDP	0.9	1.0	0.8	0.8	0.9	***	***	−0.8	−1.0
CONS	1.2	0.6	0.9	0.4	1.2	***	−1.4	−2.0	−0.7
GFCF	1.7	0.6	***	−0.4	0.9	−1.3	−0.6	−4.0	−4.5
Residential	***	−1.3	1.1	−0.3	−0.2	−2.2	−4.0	−5.5	−6.7
Other constructions	−0.1	1.3	***	−2.7	1.5	−0.9	0.2	−1.6	−0.3
Equipment goods	3.8	2.1	1.1	1.5	1.6	−1.2	***	−5.9	−8.3
Exports	4.0	4.1	0.4	1.6	0.0	0.0	***	−0.5	−9.2
Imports	5.2	2.7	1.4	0.7	***	−1.3	−1.6	−5.1	−9.1
Housing price	1.7	1.7	1.5	0.3	1.2	***	−0.3	−1.3	−2.4

Note: CONS: consumption; GFCF: gross fixed capital formation; peak reached (*).

Source: Own elaboration with data from INE (2016b) and MPW (2017).

but given the weight of construction, both investment in fixed tangible assets and gross investment reached their peak in 2007-Q2. Before the cycle of investment in equipment was reversed, the import boom stopped (2007-Q4), which preceded the beginning of the decline in exports (2008-Q2) (INE, 2016b). The price of housing meanwhile continued to grow until 2008-Q1, in turn reflecting the incidence of investment on housing prices and its role as an investment asset.

Table 1.4 reveals the central role of investment in macroeconomic dynamics, especially in construction. Although investment stops growing when adequate prospects for profitability are removed, it is investments in the field of real estate that push up prices, favoring the goal of profitability. Over a period, investment can generate profits by virtue of asset appreciation; hence this is an essential variable, which in turn explains the dynamics of imports. Therefore, this type of accumulation reveals a more complex connection between profitability, investment, and GDP and not the absence of this fundamental causality. As the emergence of the bubble can be explained by the problems of valorization and the particular Spanish context, it is necessary to transcend the macroeconomic sphere in order to explain the internal imbalances of the Spanish economy.

Internal dislocation in the dynamics of accumulation

In the Spanish case, the dynamics of accumulation have eroded profitability, but not by reducing in relative terms the use of labor power through an intensive technical change in the means of production. Quite the contrary: employment increased formidably, but it did so in those activities with reduced capacity to generate value, which in turn prevented an increase of real wages (see also Chapter 4). In this section, we proceed to analyze the internal distortions particular to this process.

The asset structure of the accumulation process, together with underlying problems of profitability and the context of membership in the EMU, led to a sectoral restructuring without which the already cited particularities of the general macroeconomic evolution cannot be understood. For this reason, we first identify the characteristics of the most dynamic economic activities in order to focus on the real estate sector.

Sectoral aspects

The sectoral imbalances in the accumulation process are manifested through the most dynamic economic activities, characterized by reduced relative levels of capital composition (labor intensive) and, therefore, the absolute level of productivity and its evolution over time, making them relatively inflationary (Tables 1.5 and 1.6).

As has been said, the growth phase was led by construction-sector and real estate activities, which went from 13.6% to 18.1% of gross value added between 1995 and 2007, as well as professional services, whose share increased concurrently from 5% to 6.5%. This growth was in turn driven by GFCF, which was increasingly used for these activities. In the first year of the period, this accounted for one-third of total investment (including residential), reaching 48% of the total in 2007. Non-residential investment diverted to unproductive activities remained

Table 1.5 Capital composition by activities, 1995–2015

Activities	Average of productive activities (%)				Annual rates of change	
			Capital–labor ratio			
	1995	*2000*	*2007*	*2015*	*1995–2007*	*2007–2015*
Construction	106.9	89.0	84.5	158.6	−1.0	13.2
Trade and reparations	39.6	45.0	51.7	51.2	3.2	4.5
Hostelry	51.1	54.6	53.4	37.2	1.3	0.0
Professional	50.0	51.5	53.3	44.1	1.5	2.2
Other services	49.4	64.6	77.9	67.3	4.8	2.7
Total productive	100.0	100.0	100.0	100.0	0.9	4.6

Activities	Capital–output ratio					
	1995	*2000*	*2007*	*2015*	*1995–2007*	*2007–2015*
Construction	95.4	91.0	88.8	146.5	1.0	9.4
Trade and reparations	49.9	60.3	68.8	68.8	4.4	2.7
Hostelry	34.0	36.7	46.7	37.2	4.3	−0.1
Professional	52.4	53.3	63.5	54.2	3.3	0.7
Other services	82.2	95.4	121.3	110.3	5.0	1.5
Total productive	100.0	100.0	100.0	100.0	1.6	2.7

Note: Capital–labor ratio (K at 2010 constant prices); capital–output ratio (K at current prices). Total productive makes reference to the ratio of productive activities.

Source: Own elaboration with data from FBBVA (2017) and INE (2016a).

Table 1.6 Sectoral comparison of productivity and price deflators, 1995–2015

Activities	% of productive activities			Annual rates of change			
	Productivity			Productivity		Prices	
	1995	2007	2015	1995–2007	2007–2015	1995–2007	2007–2015
Construction	142.19	92.88	120.54	−3.64	5.18	5.93	−1.35
Trade and reparations	71.82	74.94	77.90	0.19	2.30	2.62	−0.29
Hostelry	181.14	117.58	94.34	−3.69	−0.96	4.87	1.52
Professional	119.79	85.78	78.57	−2.90	0.70	4.46	0.73
Other services	54.14	66.59	59.43	1.58	0.37	1.85	0.88
Total productive	100	100	100	−0.16	1.81	3.19	0.28

Note: Data in percentage, sectoral level of productivity, relative to the productive sphere and annual rates of change.

Source: Own elaboration with data from FBBVA (2017) and INE (2016a).

constant during the boom, at 28% of the total flow (FBBVA, 2017), and fell during the depression, but in the case of manufacturing industries, more than two-thirds of GFCF (68% to 69%) was received by low- and medium-low-tech sectors during the boom phase (OECD, 2017). Tables 1.5 and 1.6 illustrate the behavior of construction, trade, hotels, professional services, and other services, which together generated 87.6% of total full-time employment created in the productive sphere, or 70.6% of the economy (INE, 2016a).

In relation to their capital intensity, both the K/L and K/Q ratios revealed lower-than-average levels during the housing boom, except for a notable relative increase of K/Q in 'other services', which converged with the average at the end of the expansion. Although this index experienced a considerable increase, unlike K/L, the productive results are alarmingly negative, because construction, hostelry, and professional services experienced productivity declines between 29% and 36%; that is, they fell by more than 2.9% per year. It should be noted that coking and petroleum refining, along with transportation, lost productivity, which declined by rates of 20.7% and 7.4%, respectively. Whereas commercial activity barely increased productivity (2.4% total), other services managed to improve it by 19%. In turn, apart from trade and other services, these sectors were relatively inflationary, with annual price increases of around 4.4% in the case of professional services and 5.9% in construction.

In the case of the manufacturing industry, there was a lack of production in activities of medium-high and high technological content. The value added of these branches, which had been over 7% of the total in the 1980s, was slightly over 6% in the mid-1990s, and in 2007 represented just 4.9%, although these branches continued to represent one-third of the value added in manufacturing.

In addition, while representing about two-thirds of R&D expenditures in the mid-1990s, in 2008 they accounted for only 37% of total, meaning that manufacturing lost 26 percentage points in its participation in such activities over the period (OECD, 2017).

The knock-on effect of the real estate complex

The importance of the housing bubble, along with its distorting effect on the functioning of the economy, can be explained by the huge capacity of the real estate complex (including construction and real estate services) in terms of production and employment, along with the capacity to raise financial resources. Considering the characteristics of the construction sector mentioned earlier, its carrying capacity over the whole economy has clearly been considerable. Given the explanatory power of this aspect for the dynamic we are studying, we now proceed to characterize it in quantitative terms. In order to study the relationship of this complex with the rest of the economy, an input–output analysis is used to create an aggregate matrix in just two sectors: the real estate complex and the rest of the economy. This gives us insight into its knock-on effects in terms of production and employment and, therefore, its impact on the economy in a time of crisis.[10]

Because the availability of its annual series covers the closest possible period to that under study (1995–2015), we will take the input–output tables (IOT) from the World Input-Output Database (WIOD) series.[11] The real estate complex consists of both construction and real estate activities (services sector). In 1995, the value of the Leontief inverse in the Spanish economy (characterized as described) was the following:

$$L_{1995} = \begin{pmatrix} l_{11} & l_{12} \\ l_{21} & l_{22} \end{pmatrix}_{1995} = \begin{pmatrix} 1,18 & 0,17 \\ 0,07 & 1,43 \end{pmatrix}$$

This means that the real estate complex was responsible for 7% of the total output of the rest of economy that year, whereas the non–real estate macro-sector accounted for 17% of total real estate output. If we take into account that in 1995 this represented 19% of the total output of the Spanish economy and 21% of aggregate final demand, we get an idea of the knock-on effect: a 20% fall in demand for construction in 1995 would have meant a drop in total output of $0.2 \cdot 0.19 + 0.07 \cdot 0.2 \cdot 0.81 = 3.38\% + 1.13\% = 3.82\%$. That is to say, 3.38 points due to the contribution of construction itself to the total output of the economy, plus 1.13 points due to its knock-on effect in relation to the rest of activities.

Thus, we can define the dispersion power coefficient of the real estate complex over the economy (U_1) as the sum of its weight in the total output, plus the product of l_{21} (which represents the amount of final demand required in the real estate complex for the realization of a unit of total product in the rest of the economy) by the weight of the rest of the economy in the total output. This is expressed in decimal form, and its economic meaning is the effect of an infinitesimal change in demand for the real estate complex in the total output of the economy.

Figure 1.4 shows the values of this coefficient for the period 1995–2007. The difference between this coefficient and the share of the real estate complex in the total output $X_1 / (X_1 + X_2)$ indicates its carrying capacity in relation to the rest of the economy. This capacity reached its ceiling in 2006, with 37% (whereas the real estate complex represented 33% of the total output of the economy).

From the information contained in the Leontief inverse we have calculated, in combination with employment data per unit of output (expressed as jobs per million euros in 2008), the capacity of the real estate complex can be determined in terms of employment. Figure 1.5 shows the vertically integrated employment coefficients of the real estate complex (l_1) in comparison with the direct coefficients. In the first place, it emphasizes that labor productivity (measurable as the inverse of either indicator) declined steadily until the start of the housing bubble in 2001–2002, at which point it began to increase, remaining constant during the development of the real estate bubble and until the outbreak of the crisis, in 2008, when it resumed a growth path. But throughout the development of the bubble, there was also a growing divergence between the vertically integrated employment and direct employment coefficients, which indicates that the real estate complex increased its knock-on capacity in terms of employment with respect to the rest of the economy.

Figure 1.6 gives a more explicit view of the extent to which the knock-on effect of the real estate complex in terms of employment proved significant. The difference between direct and vertically integrated jobs corresponds to indirect jobs created by the real estate complex. Thus, in 2007, the complex directly employed 2.9 million people, whereas vertically integrated employment was at 4.8 million, indicating that for each unit of direct employment, 0.7 jobs were indirectly generated.

The statistical evidence here presented shows the central character of the real estate complex in the latest expansive period of Spain's economy. This is decisive, as we shall see later, in explaining the depth of the crisis in Spain. In addition, the peculiar nature of this sector led the boom to have other negative consequences in the economy as a whole, even during the expansionary period. Some of these have been already treated; next we will discuss the others.

The impact of the housing crisis on the Spanish economy

The economic drift that fueled the expansive dynamics of the early twenty-first century and affected the real estate complex also determined the depth of the crisis when the housing bubble burst. Economic data reveal this fact at the slow pace inherent to the production of these types of goods. Although the Spanish economy officially went into recession in 2008, construction had already begun to decline in 2007, both in its share of total output and in its ability to carry the economy. The latter is shown by the fact that the dispersion power coefficient of the real estate complex U_1 (Figure 1.4), which had already begun to fall in 2007, reached levels

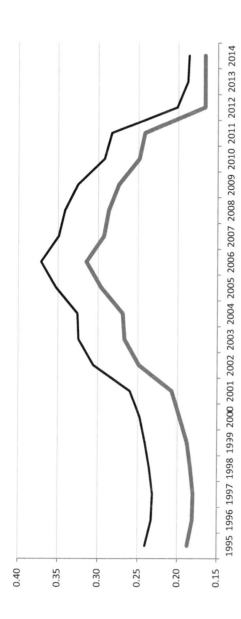

Figure 1.4 Power of dispersion of the real estate complex over the economy, 1995–2014 (coefficient in decimal form)

Source: Own elaboration with data from WIOD 2013 release (1995–2011) and 2016 release (2012–2014).

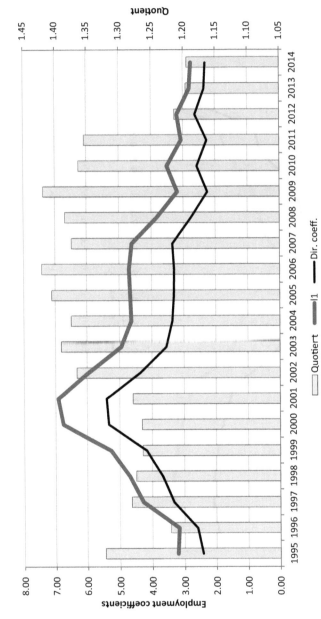

Figure 1.5 Direct and vertically integrated employment coefficients of the real estate complex, 1995–2014 (jobs per million euros in 2008 prices)

Source: Own elaboration with data from WIOD (2013 release for 1995–2011 and 2016 release for 2012–2014) and INE.

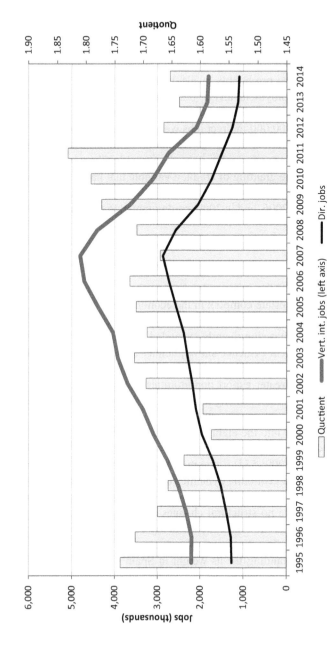

Figure 1.6 Direct and vertically integrated jobs at the real estate complex, 1995–2014 (thousands)

Source: Own elaboration with data from WIOD (2013 release for 1995–2011 and 2016 release for 2012–2014) and INE.

comparable to values that had prevailed at the beginning of the real estate bubble, indicating the extent to which linkages to the real estate complex were weakened during the crisis.

On the other hand, since 2008, following a sharp reduction in employment in the real estate complex, labor productivity increased, as measured by labor requirements both direct and vertically integrated (Figure 1.5). It is confirmed that the real estate complex reduced its carrying capacity in terms of employment with respect to the pre-bubble levels, although this figure remained high. The contraction in employment levels, both direct and vertically integrated, is shown in Figure 1.6. Between 2007 and 2015, 1.4 million direct jobs (about half of those existing) and 700,000 indirect jobs were lost. Thus, as Figure 1.7 shows, with the outbreak of the crisis, the real estate complex became the main sector for job destruction, the effects of which will be discussed in Chapter 4. This decline was also observed in the granting of credit, a variable that had been instrumental (as we shall see in Chapter 3) in inflating the real estate bubble; this had already begun to slow down in 2006, and in 2009, credit granted to the construction sector finally began to drop.

The Spanish economy, a train without a locomotive

As has become evident, the crisis unleashed on Spain's economy reduced the weight of both the real estate complex in the economy and its knock-on capacity with respect to other branches of activity. However, it should be noted that no other sector of activity has significantly expanded its capacity to drag on the rest. As the available statistical evidence shows, neither those sectors most supported by public policies during the crisis (such as the automotive industry) nor the dynamism of sectors with greater export opportunities (to be explored in Chapter 2) have been leaders in the restructuring of the productive fabric or the technological matrix.

By grouping the IOT into the eight branches of activity listed in Table 1.7 and calculating the backward and forward linkage indicators, according to Miller and Blair's methodology (2009: 555),[12] one may appreciate the role of the construction sector as a driver of economic dynamics between 2001 and 2006, the decline of its carrying capacity in 2007–2009, and the collapse of that capacity thereafter. Beyond that, there were no structural changes directly attributable to the latest expansionary phase or to the crisis: the economy suffered gradual tertiarization, causing industry (including the automotive sector) to lose capacity. Not even the hotel industry, outstanding for its weight in Spain's economy and its degree of openness, experienced an increase in its carrying capacity. In technological and productive terms, the whole economy navigated the recent economic cycle through inertia (broken only by the marked aberration of construction), suggesting deep roots that have characterized the economy for decades. For this reason, it is not possible to speak of new locomotives that might replace that which derailed when the real estate bubble burst.

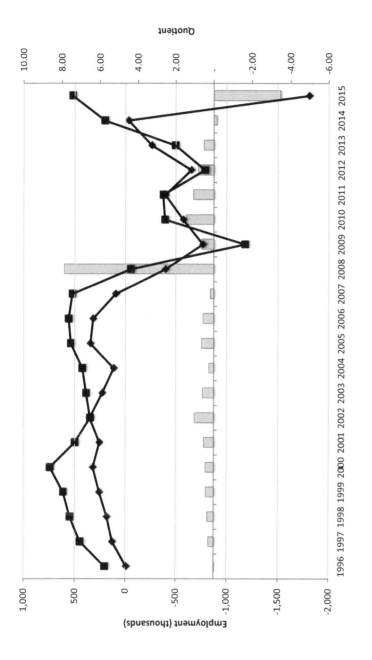

Figure 1.7 Absolute differences in the evolution of total employment and contribution of the real estate complex thereto, 1996–2015 (thousands)

Source: Own elaboration with data from INE.

Table 1.7 Backward (B_i) and forward (F_j) linkage indicators for selected sectors, 1995, 2007, and 2014

	Agriculture and mining	Food industry	Transport equipment	Other manufacturing	Electricity, gas, and water	Construction	Hotels and restaurants	Other services
Backward linkages (B_i)								
1995	0.0940	0.1060	0.0550	0.4170	0.0611	0.1671	0.0731	0.7913
2007	0.0500	0.0711	0.0490	0.3719	0.0703	0.2675	0.0641	0.8058
2014	0.0497	0.1098	0.0382	0.3034	0.1534	0.1126	0.0660	0.8920
Forward linkages (F_j)								
1995	0.0832	0.2374	0.0999	0.3892	0.0554	0.5606	0.1482	0.7506
2007	0.0387	0.1355	0.0802	0.3421	0.0510	1.0342	0.1270	0.8043
2014	0.0386	0.2194	0.0643	0.2968	0.1237	0.3394	0.1317	0.8749

Source: Own elaboration with data from WIOD (2013 release for 1995–2007 and 2016 release for 2014).

Environmental imbalances in the accumulation process

In the environmental field, during the period under review, the Spanish economy accentuated a series of trends that started in the 1950s, when it began to be externally dependent (rather than self-sufficient) in the supply of material and energy inputs, while gradually replacing renewable energy sources with non-renewable sources. The Spanish economy has thus increased its relative dependence on natural resources (and therefore its inefficiency in this regard), with a consequent increase in environmental unsustainability.

The Spanish production model has been based on non-renewable resources (80%), and 50% of natural resources used in production processes were stonework materials for construction (Carpintero and Bellver, 2013: 559). This has developed in a disperse way, with vast territorial extension, which in addition to increasing pressures for the construction of (mainly big) infrastructures, has favored transport habits based on private vehicles, which in turn has boosted the unsustainability of the production model as well as consumption in Spain during recent decades.

Added to this internal aspect of unsustainability is an external dimension, evident in the growing net flow of energy and materials to Spain. The corollary is an ecological footprint of more than 5 hectares per inhabitant, as compared to the ecologically productive surface (1.4 hectares per inhabitant) (*op.cit.*, 560). In other words, it would take three times the surface of Spain to absorb the CO_2 emissions generated within the country.

A comparison of the available indicators for Spain with EU averages shows how the housing bubble accentuated the environmental imbalance of the Spanish economy during the latest expansionary period. Thus, if in 2000 the consumption of materials per capita in Spain was already higher than the EU-28 average (according to Eurostat data), this difference was exacerbated by 2007 so that the average resident in Spain consumed 25% more materials than the average European.

The crisis, especially deep in the construction sector, reversed these proportions so that in 2014 the average Spanish resident consumed just 70% as much as the average European, although in this and the other environmental indicators considered, the effect of the crisis in the EU as a whole was a reduction in such consumption. The collapse of the building sector also led to an improvement in the efficiency of resource use (according to Eurostat data), which had been consistently growing at below the European average.[13] The indicators for energy consumption and CO_2 emissions showed a markedly greater increase than those of the EU-15. Again, the depth and character of the crisis in Spain moved these indicators into a pattern similar to that of Europe, with sharp reductions in 2008–2009 and a progressively downward path ever since. The crisis has also led to a collapse in the use of non-renewable materials, as well as of certain inputs typically related to the real estate complex, such as steel and cement. According to data from the Bank of Spain (BoS), the latter was consumed at around 20 million tons in 1993, reaching more than 50 million tons in 2006, only to fall below 25 million tons just two years later. In 2015, total cement consumption stood at 11.4 million tons.

As such, the crisis has led to some improvement in environmental indicators; however, this has not responded to the emergence of a new productive or technological pattern (as noted in the previous section), but rather to a quantity effect caused by the collapse of the very activity that drove the latest expansionary cycle: construction. In addition, although the crisis has partially and temporarily reversed these trends, the process of acquiring materials and transforming the environment that fed the latest real estate bubble stands in contrast to possible future movement towards a less environmentally predatory economy.

Conclusions

Our analysis of the accumulation of capital is relevant insofar as it has addressed the sphere of surplus generation (a central aspect in capitalism), and this provides the basis from which we will undertake subsequent chapters on aspects such as external relations, finance, the labor market, and the distribution of income, all of which can be understood only if the fundamentals of the Spanish economy's growth model have been deeply and fully grasped.

As we have seen, residential assets in Spain became vehicles for valorization, with an average annual increase of 12% between 1999 and 2007, which in 2002–2005 ranged from 13% to 17% annually. That increase, linked to a price effect, was closely related to the growing weight of investment in construction assets, which accounted for more than two-thirds of the total in the period under study. Nonetheless, the rate of accumulation of non-residential (so-called 'productive') net capital was remarkably intense, 4.5% per year in 1995–2007, but falling to less than 1.5% during 2008–15.

The capital–wage labor ratio did not increase during the growth phase, although due to extension of the degree of salarization, the total capital–labor ratio rose by almost 12%, a substantially reduced level in any case. In addition, the capital–output ratio increased in a limited way, by barely 21% during the boom (although, paradoxically, to a greater extent than capital–labor). As a result, productivity per full-time worker experienced a staggering decline of -1.9% during a 12-year period of uninterrupted expansion. Related to this productive decline was the relative increase in the capital stock price index, which translated to a drop in the P_{yk} of 4.6% in 2000–2007.

In short, all this constitutes a strongly distorted dynamic of the process of accumulation, reflected in terms of profitability. On the one hand, the volume of surplus in real terms grew during 2000–2006 at a rate equivalent to little more than half of the rate of increase in the mid-to-late 1990s, peaking in 2006, two years before the outbreak of the crisis. By 2015, gross profit had still not recovered, being 4% lower than the peak. On the other hand, the rate of profit during the period fell by 40%. However, this exceptional deterioration in profitability was offset by a proportionately larger drop in interest rates, which in turn favored the appreciation of construction assets, and thus occluding the underlying deterioration of profitability.

This paradoxical evolution justifies a reconsideration of the sectoral structure of the process of accumulation, unavoidably affected by the largest real estate bubble in Spain's history. In addition, the impact of the latest housing bubble remains fundamental to understanding the boom in both the material requirements of the economy and its waste emissions, key elements in the environmental unsustainability of the Spanish economy. The worsening and then subsequent improvement of these indicators can be explained to a great extent by the rise and fall of the construction sector in the period examined. In any case, the environmental unsustainability is still a structural feature of the Spanish growth model.

Given all of this, it can be said that the crisis has been characterized by an insufficient capacity to generate surplus, which has in turn served as the basis for further distortions. Consequently, full emergence from the recession will not occur until the ability to generate surplus is raised to a level appropriate to the current stock of capital. The atypical upward trajectories of the composition of capital, labor productivity, and wages from 2007 do not reflect a recomposition of the conditions of valorization. On the contrary, these are developments particular to the crisis, due to the large increase in unemployment and the decrease in the use of installed capacity. However, the rate of profit remains low, and high levels of debt persist.

This analysis has illuminated a number of implications for other dimensions of the Spanish economy, among which we highlight the following:

i) The external insertion of the Spanish economy, which is examined in the next chapter, has been determined by the level of productive development, but also by how integration into the monetary union has influenced the speculative boom, being based on an incoherent exchange rate parity which has favored the profitability of non-tradable productive activities. Therefore, this model of accumulation has perpetuated the technological dependency of Spain.

ii) Interest rates, the evolution of which will be analyzed in Chapter 3, excessively reduced by incorporation into the EMU, served to offset underlying problems of profitability and favored (but did not create) access to resources for investment, productive or otherwise. In the same way, their increase with the crisis was consistent with the lower productive capacity of the Spanish economy, as well as being functional to restructuring, both in terms of total social capital (bankruptcies, depreciation of assets, etc.) and in the geopolitics of monetary union (geographical polarization). In other words, financial expansion has been closely related to this valorization framework.

iii) Wage regression, the depth of which will be addressed in Chapters 4 and 5, has been essential for the speculative real estate model, insofar as it has favored the profitability of capital in a context in which the latter was facing structural limits to its growth. At the same time, this is one consequence of a type of growth that has not developed productivity and has in turn prevented wage increases. Thus, both the precariousness of labor and inequality have an objective foundation in the valorization process.

In conclusion, from the perspective of the working class, any project toward transformation must lay the foundations of an alternative growth model to increase productivity and generate a basis for better living conditions of the population at large. In this sense, the proposal to nationalize basic sectors of the economy is an essential centerpiece for the long term. Only in this way will it be possible to change the type of external insertion and the role of Spain in the international division of labor, thus allowing for better wages and a sufficient social protection system.

Notes

1 Author names are given in alphabetical order, as both share equal responsibility for this chapter.
2 Although the crisis erupted in mid-2008, a significant change in the evolution of several relevant variables was observed in 2007, which is why it was decided to establish that year as the end of the period of expansion. The depression lasted until 2013, with a very slight recovery up to 2015, so some indicators of this period are referenced until 2013.
3 It should be noted that calculations of the rate of profit and its determinants in this chapter exclude finance and real estate, government, and social services. Given the importance these have in an economy like Spain, we can thus better see the underlying profitability of capital there.
4 However, one of the implications of the integration of Spain into the EMU has been the adoption of an exceedingly small interest rate in relation to productive development so that this variable has functioned as a clearly exogenous factor that promoted a distorted type of capital accumulation.
5 It should be noted that the dynamics of the process of accumulation fed back into the bubble, in that intensive low-qualification labor sectors were stimulated, prompting an influx of immigrants that increased Spain's population substantially, given the low birth rates of the native population. Population growth went from less than 0.3% annually in the early 1990s to over 1% in 2001, and it fluctuated around 1.7% to 1.8% per year since 2003 (AMECO, 2017).
6 Segura (2012: 33) emphasizes the strong link between transport infrastructure projects and speculative urban developments and points out that Spain is the second nation in the world in terms of kilometers of high-speed rail (although 'we only have a fifth of the travelers of France, or 7% of those in Japan') and the third with more kilometers of motorways and highways.
7 In an historical perspective, this rate of accumulation has not been especially remarkable, because it surpasses only that of the 1984–1991 expansion cycle (4.2%), being lower than that of the 1965–1974 period (7.7%) and even that of the recessive decade of 1974–1984 (4.9%).
8 Although the mass of profit in relation to GDP increased by 33.2% in 1995–2007, when viewed in relation to capital it is 5.3 points lower (that is, it increased by 25.8%).
9 Unlike in the United States, in Spain there is no disaggregated quarterly statistical basis that allows for analysis of the expression of the surplus used in this document to calculate the rate of profit; thus, we must limit ourselves to investment.
10 In our case, the matrix of technical coefficients has been calculated first and the necessary transformations have been carried out: aggregation of sectors until reaching a matrix of 2 × 2 dimension in which the real estate complex relates to the rest of the economy, obtaining the Leontief inverse. For a detailed description of the procedure for matrix aggregation, see Miller and Blair (2009: 16).

11 Moreover, because we try to study the underlying technological matrix, we will use only the internal magnitudes of the IOT, not the imported aspects.
12 The coefficient of backward linkages of each branch has been determined as the sum of the elements of the same row of the weighted Leontief inverse multiplied by its weight in the total output. The forward link coefficient has been determined as the sum of the elements of the same column, also multiplied by the relative weight of the sector.
13 Carpintero (2015: 73) uses a broader period of analysis to conclude that 'the Spanish economy used more than twice the energy and materials per unit of GDP at the beginning of the twenty-first century than it used in 1960'. This calls into question the supposed 'dematerialization' of the economy which, according to many, should have taken place thanks to new technologies.

References

AMECO (2017): *Annual Macro-Economic Database*, European Commission, Economic and Financial Affairs.
Bank of Spain (BoS) (2017a): *Economic Indicators*, Madrid: Bank of Spain. Available at: www.bde.es/webbde/es/estadis/infoest/indeco.html
_____. (2017b): *Statistical Bulletin*, Madrid: Bank of Spain. Available at: www.bde.es/webbde/es/estadis/infoest/bolest.html
_____. (2017c): *Summary Indicators*, Madrid: Bank of Spain. Available at: www.bde.es/webbde/en/estadis/infoest/sindi.html
_____. (2017d): *Central Balance Sheet Data Office: Non Financial Corporations*, Madrid: Bank of Spain. Available at: www.bde.es/webbde/en/estadis/infoest/bolest15.html
Bellod, J.F. (2007): 'Crecimiento y especulación inmobiliaria en la economía española', *Principios: Estudios de Economía Política*, 8, pp. 59–84.
Carpintero, O. (dir.) (2015): *El metabolismo económico regional español*, Madrid: FUHEM Ecosocial.
Carpintero, O. and Bellver, J. (2013): '¿Es posible la sostenibilidad ambiental de la economía española?', in Worldwatch Institute (ed.), *Informe sobre la situación del mundo 2013: ¿Es aún posible lograr la sostenibilidad?*, Madrid: FUHEM Ecosocial/Icaria.
Cuadrado-Roura, J.R. (dir.) (2010): *El sector construcción en España. Análisis, perspectivas y propuestas*, Madrid: Colegio Libre de Eméritos.
Fernández, R. and García, C. (2016): 'Wheels Within Wheels Within Wheels: The Importance of Capital Inflows in the Origin of the Spanish Financial Crisis', *PERI Working Paper*, 413, Amherst: University of Massachusetts.
FBBVA (2017): *El stock y los servicios del capital en España y su distribución territorial y sectorial (1964–2013)*. Madrid: Fundación BBVA/Ivie. Available at: www.fbbva.es/TLFU/microsites/stock09/fbbva_stock08_index.html
García, J.L. and Myro, R. (dirs.) (2015): *Lecciones de economía española*, Pamplona: Civitas.
Gotham, K.F. (2006): 'The Secondary Circuit of Capital Reconsidered: Globalization and the U.S. Real Estate Sector', *American Journal of Sociology*, 112 (1), pp. 231–275.
Harvey, D. (1973): *Social Justice and the City*, London: Edward Arnold.
INE (2016a): *Annual Spanish National Accounts. Series from 1995. Base 2010*, Madrid: National Statistics Institute.
_____ (2016b): *Quarterly Spanish National Accounts: Base 2010*, Madrid: National Statistics Institute.

Mateo, J.P. (2017): 'Theory and Practice of Crisis in Political Economy: The Case of the Great Recession in Spain', *Working Paper* (*Department of Economics, The New School for Social Research*), 15/2017.

Miller, R.E. and Blair, P.D. (2009): *Input-Output Analysis. Foundations and Extensions*, Cambridge: Cambridge University Press.

Ministry of Public Works and Transport (MPW) (2017): *Información estadística: Valor tasado de la vivienda*, Madrid: Ministry of Public Works and Transport.

OECD (2017): *Statistical Databases*, Paris: Organisation for Economic Co-Operation and Development.

Rodríguez, E. and López, I. (2010): *Fin de ciclo. Financiarización territorio y sociedad de propietarios en la onda larga del capitalismo hispano (1959–2010)*, Madrid: Traficantes de Sueños.

Segura, F. (2012): *Infraestructuras de transporte y crisis: Grandes obras en tiempos de recortes sociales*, Madrid: Libros en Acción.

Shaikh, A. (2016): *Capitalism: Competition, Conflict, Crises*, New York: Oxford University Press.

World Input-Output Database (various years): *National Input-Output Tables*. Available at: www.wiod.org

2 Spain's external insertion

Peripheral or not?

Manuel Gracia and María José Paz[1]

Introduction

The main objective of this chapter is to analyze the evolution of the external insertion, in terms of both trade and production, of the Spanish economy. Clearly, this insertion is largely determined by characteristics of the pattern of accumulation and by the sectoral structure of the economy, the fundamentals of which were analyzed in the previous chapter. In addition, structural imbalances in the external sector of Spain's economy have promoted, and been amplified by, the dynamics of external indebtedness, as will be analyzed in Chapter 3.

In order to develop our objective, we first consider whether it is possible (and relevant) to speak of 'modalities of insertion' and whether we can situate Spain in one such modality. In this chapter, we assume that it is indeed possible and that the various modalities are expressions of the uneven development and hierarchical structure of the capitalist world economy, with international economic relations of domination and dependence expressed both worldwide and in smaller regions. We suggest that this hierarchical view and the mechanisms on which it is based constitute the core of a center–periphery (C-P) approach, although this aspect has been sometimes forgotten in analyses of C-P in Europe, making it difficult to find consensus on what precisely characterizes the periphery (Lapavitsas et al., 2010; Fitoussi, 2010; Álvarez et al., 2013). For the purposes of this chapter, the assumption of a C-P approach allows us to assess whether, in the wake of changes experienced by the Spanish economy in terms of international trade and production relations, there persist elements of vulnerability inherent to 'peripheral insertion'. In order to identify those elements, we consider specific literature that has developed a C-P approach, especially in the decades following the Second World War.[2] We do not attempt a comprehensive review, but synthetically examine the literature for contributions that are key to the development of our analysis.

Initial considerations of the C-P binomial in the analysis of economic processes can be found in Sombart, Marx, or Bujarin (García et al., 2007), but it was Prebisch who consolidated this concept into a fundamental basis for analysis of Latin American structuralism, starting from the rejection of mutual benefit in international trade relations. This structuralist-ECLAC vision (ECLAC being the

Economic Commission for Latin America and the Caribbean, where it largely developed) rested on three essential ideas:

i) The existence of differentiated productive structures between the center (homogeneous and diversified) and the periphery (heterogeneous and specialized).
ii) The relationship of these structures through the international division of labor, performing different and complementary functions.
iii) The asymmetry of relations between the center and the periphery, perpetuating the disparity among its productive structures.

The C-P approach eventually led to the identification of trade relations as the chief exponent of asymmetric relations in the world economy (Martínez, 2011). However, the original feature of this approach was to take as a starting point and key element technical progress and the productivity gains derived therefrom, the distribution of which was analytically linked with the international division of labor (Di Filippo, 1998: 175).[3] Articulation of these internal and external elements established the basis for a hierarchically structured world system in which peripheral insertion was characterized by a primary-export pattern with a dependence on imports of manufactures.

The structuralist C-P approach, although with modifications, continued via two routes. First, it evolved during the 1960s and 1970s by way of dependency approaches, where the dependence on foreign capital takes center stage as a distinctive factor for the periphery. Second, structuralist C-P persisted in the world economy approach and in nuanced dependency contributions that served as a bridge to that end (Evans, 1979; Chase-Dunn and Rubinson, 1977). This second path has remained more active to present day, highlighting two distinctive facets: its shading of the determinism of the more radical dependency approaches (admitting the possibility of some development in conjunction with a peripheral position) and the introduction of the concept of a commodity chain, understood as a 'network of labor and production processes whose result is a finished commodity' (Hopkins and Wallerstein, 1977: 112). This concept proved pioneering in the connection of production and trade internationalization within a single unit of analysis (a commodity chain) and in situating C-P relations into that unit of analysis.

Later works under a different denomination (global commodity chains) have focused on identifying hierarchical (governance) structures which vary according to the type of activity. Nonetheless, in all such cases it is clear that control of the chain by transnational corporations (TNCs) is no longer limited to subsidiaries, but also, and increasingly, may extend to a network of suppliers. These relations of power are connected via specialization patterns within the chain in which the use and control of technology continues to be a determinant in generating situations of dominance/dependence for some firms vis-à-vis others (Gereffi et al., 2005). Most relevant is not merely whether an increase (decrease) in trade and production relations occurs in the context of commodity chains, but rather the *position* occupied along such chains.

In short, these latter contributions intended to digest the economic transformations that have taken place in the world economy since the 1970s. In particular, the industrialization of certain peripheral economies (New International Division of Labor) and the offshoring of production, both of which rendered obsolete the original formulation based on primary-export patterns and foreign direct investment (FDI) inflows as the unique expressions of foreign capital dominance. However, despite changes to the forms, a hierarchical pattern persists in the internationalization of production and trade, making it possible to verify different modalities of peripheral insertion, among the features of which we emphasize two[4]:

i) The control by foreign capital of sectors of greater technological intensity and greater export dynamism in the economy; this control is verified not only through FDI, but also through the network of (national) companies that are part of the commodity chain;

ii) A pattern of commercial insertion in which, despite the increasing role of intra-industrial trade, it is possible to identify a technologically dependent specialization that generates strong imbalances.

As we will see throughout this chapter, these basic ideas allow us to adequately understand the external insertion of the Spanish economy. In the section that follows we analyze Spain's production insertion so that in the third section we may better understand the country's international trade relations. In the fourth section, we conclude by discussing the scope and limitations of the changes experienced by way of Spain's external insertion in the pre-crisis period and once the internal devaluation was introduced during the crisis.

The Spanish economy in international production

Here our objective is to analyze the participation of the Spanish economy in international production. Given the importance of FDI in this section, it is necessary to make two prior clarifications. First, FDI has a production but also a financial dimension. Regarding the latter, FDI is equivalent to a source of external savings, such as portfolio investment, through which an economy carrying an external deficit can be financed. This financial dimension connects with the contents of the next chapter and so will not be analyzed here.

Second, it should be noted that FDI flows have traditionally been used as an indicator of the expansion, presence, and control of production by TNCs. However, two facts make the validity of this indicator less relevant:

i) Increasingly, a portion of FDI flows stray from their supposed orientation toward production, including those funds channeled through holding companies, in particular Foreign-Securities Holding Entities (in Spanish, *Empresas de Tenencia de Valores Extranjeros*, ETVEs) or operations of exchange of stock between subsidiaries of the same company;

ii)   As we have already pointed out, the internationalization of production and its control by large TNCs is increasingly developed in ways that do not require FDI, such as through subcontracting, franchising, service contracts, etc. (UNCTAD, 2012).

General trends in FDI flows

Analyzing the role of the Spanish economy in global FDI flows requires considering both inflows and outflows. The joint analysis of both issues, and comparison with trends in surrounding countries, allows us to identify three fundamental features in the evolution of these flows.[5]

First, in the last three decades, Spain has ceased to be fundamentally a recipient country – a feature typical of the periphery, instead becoming an investor. Not only have outflows increased more than inflows (except in the post-crisis period), but in 2014, the stock of Spanish FDI abroad was higher than the stock of FDI in Spain (Figure 2.1). This 'new' net position has had implications on the income balance of the Spanish economy, as income from the repatriation of profits has increased, especially after the crisis. Subsequently, this formidable change has been interpreted as a result of notable improvements in the external insertion of the Spanish economy (Fernández-Otheo and Myro, 2015: 33) (an interpretation that will be reviewed throughout this section).

As a second fundamental feature, focusing only on net flows without highlighting ETVE operations, we find the existence of a differentiated pattern between the 1995–2007 and 2008–2014 periods, with reverse trends of growth and decline. Indeed, if we discount the two mega-mergers of Vodafone and Endesa in 2000 and 2007, respectively, the data show that the capacity of the Spanish economy to attract FDI (without ETVE) has been higher in the post-crisis period (€15,273 billion on annual average) than in the previous period (€6,557 billion).[6] There has been a somewhat opposite dynamic in outflows (€11,372 billion on annual average between 2008 and 2015, compared to €26,770 billion between 1995 and 2007).[7] Thus, in the wake of the crisis, Spain now occupies a position of net recipient of investment, narrowing the distance between inward and outward stock that had opened, in favor of the latter, throughout the previous three decades.

The third highlighted issue is that, unlike in the case of trade, as we shall see, Spain has maintained a higher degree of insertion in the world economy via FDI (measured by its share in the global stock, according to United Nations Conference on Trade and Development [UNCTAD] data) than the degree that would correspond to the size of its economy. As a host economy, the average value of Spanish participation is close to 3%, and as a home economy 2.3%, but with a clear upward trend interrupted only temporarily at the beginning of the crisis. This fact reinforces the arguments of those who maintain, as we have pointed out, that Spanish external insertion has experienced marked improvement, at least through its participation in international production.

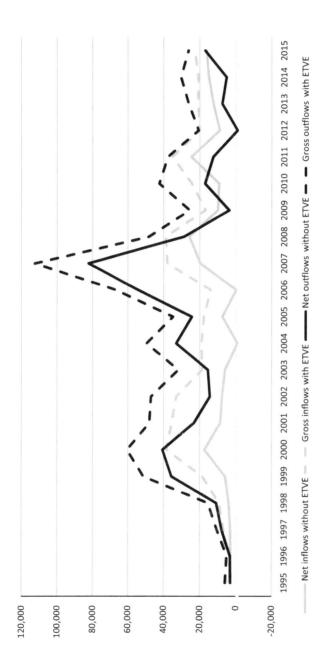

Figure 2.1 FDI: inflows and outflows (millions of euro)

Source: Own elaboration with data from Datainvext.

Dependence on or interdependence with foreign capital?

We begin this section by examining whether there has been an increase or decrease in the relative importance of foreign capital in the Spanish economy and in the main sectors on which it is based and by stating whether participation and control by foreign capital have occurred in key sectors. To do this, we use two fundamental criteria: technological intensity and export projection. Thus, insertion will be considered 'more dependent' the greater the relative importance of foreign capital in high-tech sectors, and the greater the export dynamism of the sectors with a greater presence of FDI.

Analyzing the relative importance of FDI by relating it to fundamental variables, such as GDP or gross fixed capital formation (GFCF), and using data from UNCTAD, we can draw a comparison between Spain and other European countries. As shown in Table 2.1, the relative importance of FDI to Spain has been somewhat higher than the European Union (EU) average, even in the period 2008–2014 (a period which includes the economies of Eastern Europe, where the presence of foreign capital is high).

Although these data are already illustrative, they remain too general because the importance of the FDI stock and the presence of foreign affiliates is highly unequal in terms of economy sectors. In fact, the stock of FDI has been concentrated into very few areas. Only 3 (electricity and gas supply, non-metallic mineral production, and trade) of the 87 sectors included in the classification represented a third of all FDI stock in 2014.[8]

On the other hand, focusing on manufacturing, there is a significant absence of high-tech sectors among the main recipients of FDI (computer or optical equipment), which are (accordingly) sectors of low importance within Spanish industry.

Table 2.1 FDI indicators, 1990–2014

	FDI inward stock/GDP			FDI inflows/GFCF		
	1990–1999	2000–2007	2008–2014	1990–1999	2000–2007	2008–2014
Developed economies	**12.6**	**23.5**	**31.9**	**4.9**	**9.5**	**7.8**
European Union	14.5	29.7	43.7	7.2	15.7	9.8
France	17.5	18.0	24.6	7.6	5.6	4.3
Germany	12.9	16.6	20.4	2.4	12.2	4.2
Italy	6.1	12.7	16.2	1.8	6.9	3.2
Spain	16.3	34.4	45.7	8.0	13.9	10.6
United Kingdom	15.2	22.9	24.0	5.0	6.0	6.6
Developing economies	**15.0**	**24.5**	**26.7**	**7.8**	**11.4**	**8.6**
Total	**13.0**	**23.7**	**29.9**	**5.5**	**10.1**	**8.4**

Source: Own elaboration with data from UNCTAD.

However, although the FDI stock in these sectors is low compared to others, the importance of foreign affiliates within these sectors is relatively high. Instead, the stock of FDI is concentrated in medium-intensity technological activities (manufacturing of motor vehicles, chemicals, and pharmaceuticals), in which the relative importance of foreign affiliates is also very high, and this has been clearly reinforced following the crisis. This means that the presence of foreign capital has been accentuated in those manufactures within Spanish industry that are of higher technological intensity and in which there is a strong dependence on foreign capital in terms of both employment and value added (Table 2.2). In short, throughout the period, there have been no substantial changes in the sectoral distribution of foreign capital in manufactures, which explains why no transformations in the production structure have been stimulated by foreign capital, confirming thereby the structural stagnation verified in the previous chapter.

Table 2.2 Participation of foreign companies' subsidiaries, 2008–2013 (% of total companies)

	2008	2009	2010	2011	2012	2013
	Persons employed					
INDUSTRY	15.30	15.10	19.80	20.90	22.20	21.40
Extractive industries, energy, and water	5.30	5.10	14.80	15.50	17.10	13.70
Food, beverages, and tobacco	10.90	10.50	12.80	13.10	13.20	12.60
Textiles, clothing, leather, and footwear	3.50	3.90	4.70	4.50	4.50	4.30
Wood and cork, paper and graphic arts	6.70	6.30	9.50	10.20	10.90	11.40
Chemical and pharmaceutical industry	29.00	28.80	36.50	36.40	39.70	40.30
Rubber and plastics	30.90	30.80	35.80	35.90	38.40	37.30
Non-metallic mineral products	9.70	10.60	14.80	15.20	16.50	17.20
Metallurgy and metal products	8.00	8.00	9.90	11.60	12.30	12.80
Electrical, electronic, and optical equipment	28.10	27.10	32.90	33.50	36.00	34.80
Machinery and mechanical equipment	19.00	16.80	23.70	23.30	25.30	25.40
Transport equipment	55.20	52.40	65.20	67.70	67.80	67.60
TOTAL	**10.80**	**10.90**	**12.10**	**12.40**	**12.80**	**13.30**
	Value added					
INDUSTRY	20.80	20.90	29.70	30.50	32.30	32.30
Extractive industries, energy, and water	9.50	12.30	30.40	30.00	31.80	27.50
Food, beverages, and tobacco	20.90	18.80	21.00	20.30	21.70	19.20
Textiles, clothing, leather, and footwear	5.30	5.20	6.30	6.60	6.80	7.20
Wood and cork, paper and graphic arts	9.70	9.40	13.60	14.20	16.40	18.60
Chemical and pharmaceutical industry	33.70	34.20	42.70	42.80	49.80	52.30
Rubber and plastics	36.50	37.60	45.60	47.40	51.10	50.90
Non-metallic mineral products	13.90	16.00	22.50	22.70	25.40	25.70
Metallurgy and metal products	14.60	14.30	17.10	18.50	16.20	19.80
Electrical, electronic, and optical equipment	32.50	34.60	38.60	41.70	43.80	44.90
Machinery and mechanical equipment	23.30	22.60	31.40	30.50	33.40	35.20
Transport equipment	57.90	54.60	69.40	71.80	70.70	75.20
TOTAL	**16.20**	**16.50**	**19.90**	**20.70**	**21.60**	**22.40**

Source: Own elaboration with data from FILINT and INE.

Together with the earlier analysis, the relative importance of foreign capital must also be valued for its link with exports, especially given the internal devaluation strategy assumed by the government after the crisis. According to Alvarez and Fernández-Otheo (2015), in 2011, foreign subsidiaries were responsible for almost 40% of exports of manufactures (30% for the economy as a whole), an aggregate figure that conceals significant differences among sectors. Two of the aforementioned sectors, manufacturing of motor vehicles and pharmaceuticals, claim the highest shares of foreign capital in exports (75% and 63%, respectively).

In short, the data are clear: although the presence of foreign capital has been uneven among different activities, it has been high in sectors with more technological intensity and in the most dynamic manufacturing sectors in terms of exports.

On the other hand, taking into account that the international fragmentation of production dominates most of the sectors mentioned, part of the activity of domestic firms and their exports is closely linked to the control of global (regional) production chains by leading firms through various forms of subcontracting. This control, which implies the ability to decide who produces and what is produced, is not reflected in the indicators analyzed earlier. Nevertheless, this is currently (and increasingly) the method being chosen by TNCs to internationalize production.

The indicators for Spanish participation in global production chains show that the sectors with the greatest presence of foreign capital have been precisely those most integrated into these chains (Solaz, 2016), which is consistent with our findings on the links between foreign capital and export dynamism. However, the relevant aspect is not only the *degree* but rather the *type* of participation. In this sense, the literature attempts to differentiate between articulation based on the import of inputs (backward) and articulation based on the provision of inputs to other economies (forward). The data in Table 2.3 illustrate the type of Spain's

Table 2.3 Trade indicators of participation in global production chains, 1995 and 2011

	1995			2011		
	Backward (a)[1]	Forward (b)[2]	Participation index (a + b)	Backward (a)[1]	Forward (b)[2]	Participation index (a + b)
Czech Republic	30.5	17.4	47.9	45.3	19.6	64.9
France	17.3	17.9	35.2	25.1	21.9	47.0
Germany	14.9	20.7	35.6	25.5	24.1	49.6
Italy	17.2	15.4	32.6	26.5	21.1	47.6
Japan	5.6	23.8	29.4	14.7	32.8	47.5
South Korea	22.3	17.1	39.4	41.7	20.5	62.2
Spain	19.2	14.3	33.5	26.9	19.7	46.6
USA	11.5	19.4	30.9	15.0	24.9	39.9
OECD	22.3	16.5	38.9	29.7	22.5	52.2
Non OECD	20.1	14.6	34.8	24.1	21.9	46.0

Notes: (1) Foreign value added embodied in exports as a percentage of total gross exports; (2) Domestic value added embodied in foreign exports as a percentage of total gross exports.

Source: Own elaboration with data from TiVA database.

participation, clearly highlighting that the country has a backward component (import dependency) higher than the forward component, which is below the average of both OECD and non-OECD countries. This type of articulation will be discussed in more detail in the next section.

Following the analysis of global chains, we recall that, within those chains, power and control relationships are directly related to the specializations of the different firms. Therefore, what is relevant from the point of view of this chapter is that control is verified in the capacity to decide what is produced and where it is produced, which consequently affects trade flows. Analysis of these flows makes it possible to grasp the different positions within the chain and to see how power allows for organization of the fragmentation of production, leading to the improvement of competitiveness.

As an illustration, we apply this analysis at the national level to the European automotive sector, in which Spain holds a high share (being the fifth-largest producer). In this chain, it is possible to relate the position as a supplier of final goods (export competitiveness) with the position as a buyer of intermediate goods. As shown in Figures 2.2[9] and 2.3,[10] German dominance has been indisputable, with Germany clearly leveraging its position as a buyer of intermediate goods to achieve the best position as a supplier of final goods. Spain, although among the five main producers, has maintained a better position as a buyer of intermediate goods than as a supplier of final goods, which reveals a more input-dependent participation in relation to its share in exports of final goods.

Finally, before closing this section, it is necessary to return to the analysis of FDI outflows and their significance to the external-insertion modality of the Spanish economy. In order to do this, it is necessary to address Spain's links with production and international trade. In particular, we wonder if outflows have been the result of the process of production diversification and technological upgrading that has culminated in the internationalization of Spanish firms, as counterpart to the presence of foreign capital in key Spanish sectors.

As explained in Chapter 1, there has been no process of structural change in which activities of greater technological complexity have gained prominence so that FDI from Spain can hardly be the culmination of such a process. And this is the case regardless of whether it reflects the financial, technological, or managerial strengths of certain companies in which FDI outflows are certainly very concentrated (Guillén and García-Canal, 2011). In fact, as in neighboring countries, these outflows are testimony to the process of capital centralization rather than a process of internationalization of production with trade links.

This is evident in the sectoral distribution of FDI outflows (Table 2.4), as we find that the main sectors have been services, such as telecommunications (mainly in the period 1995–2007), or finance (2008–2015), with horizontal investments; which is to say, investments with little impact on trade flows. Investments made from the manufacturing sector have had a much smaller share, being more dynamic during the 2000–2007 period than afterwards.

If we look at the shares of the different branches within manufacturing sectors, certain changes can be verified when comparing the 2001–2007 period with

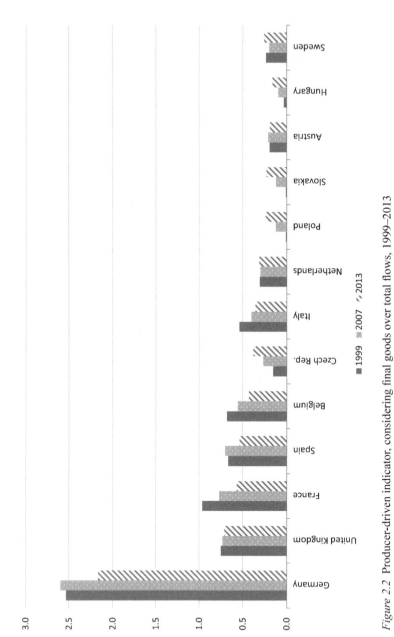

Figure 2.2 Producer-driven indicator, considering final goods over total flows, 1999–2013

Source: Own elaboration with data from Comext and Eurostat.

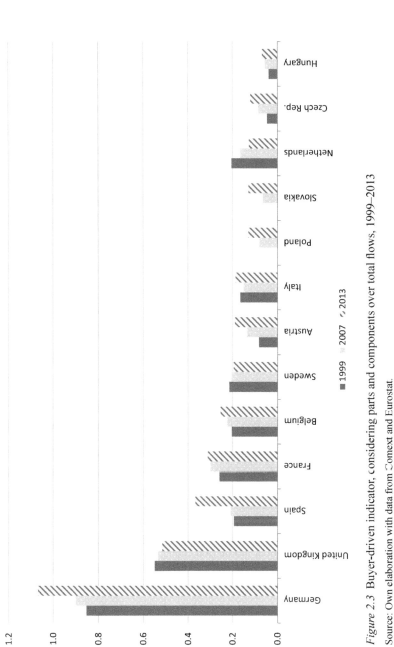

Figure 2.3 Buyer-driven indicator, considering parts and components over total flows, 1999–2013

Source: Own elaboration with data from Comext and Eurostat.

Table 2.4 Sectoral distribution of FDI net outflows (without ETVE), 1995–2015 (selected sectors; %)

	1995–2000	2001–2007	2008–2015
Total industry	**12.79**	**24.92**	**13.98**
Metallurgy	1.10	3.03	3.55
Beverages	0.58	0.68	2.77
Motor vehicles, trailers	0.93	2.93	2.10
Electrical equipment	0.44	−0.29	2.05
Food	0.98	1.91	2.01
Pharmaceutical industry	0.04	3.89	0.97
Chemical industry	1.07	3.66	0.89
Non-metallic mineral products	4.65	3.48	0.47
Computer and electronic products	−0.03	0.15	0.14
Textiles	0.03	0.19	0.04
Leather and footwear	0.03	0.04	−0.01
Wood and cork other than furniture	0.42	0.20	−0.44
Clothing	0.00	0.22	−0.49
Metal products	0.12	0.27	−0.53
Tobacco	1.42	0.81	−1.00
Energy and water supply	**9.16**	**10.63**	**5.34**
Construction	**0.86**	**4.55**	**6.19**
Information and communications	**20.16**	**20.76**	**6.53**
Financial services and insurance	**26.75**	**22.72**	**51.75**
Real state	**0.34**	**1.03**	**3.59**

Source: Own elaboration with data from Datainvex.

2008–2015. During the former, the main outflows were in medium or medium-high technological sectors (almost the same as in the case of inflows: chemical, pharmaceutical, motor vehicles). This concordance between the sectors of origin and destination is explained by the fact that a high percentage of FDI outflows in these activities (up to 70% of the stock in 2010; Fernández-Otheo and Myro, 2015: 293–299) are carried out by subsidiaries of foreign companies. In addition, the activities inside global production chains boost the internationalization of suppliers in the hands of big leading companies of those chains.

Since the crisis (2008–2015), the share of manufactures has fallen, and its sectoral distribution has turned to activities of lower technological content, where the presence and control of global production chains by Spanish companies is greater. Also highlighted is the increase in construction and real estate activities, confirming the connection between the internationalization of Spanish companies and the structure of production.

In short, despite the boom in FDI outflows, there has been limited presence by Spanish TNCs in the control of international production with greater technological content, which is consistent with the characteristics of the Spanish production model and the changes it has experienced in the last two decades. This is a fundamental question for assessing improvement in the rankings of investor countries, and so we conclude that the increase in FDI outflows cannot be valued qualitatively as the transition to a situation of interdependence in the control of the international production. This analysis must next be complemented by analysis of the trade flows with which FDI outflow is intrinsically connected.

Trade pattern

After analyzing the trend and sectoral characteristics of Spain's position in terms of international production, in this section we show the main characteristics of the country's trade insertion, with the purpose of linking both dimensions and obtaining an overall picture of the external insertion of the Spanish economy.

Spain's economy has been characterized by a structural and pro-cyclical current account deficit, accelerated during the 2000s, largely due to the dynamics of external overindebtedness (analyzed in Chapter 3) which reached a peak in 2007 and has been corrected since then.[11] Most of the deficit growth corresponded to trade of goods, the balance of which followed a similar evolution in trend and volume to that of the current account. As countervailing effects, exports of services increased, and there was also a slight increase in the capital account surplus, but these were nevertheless insufficient to balance the total account. From some approaches, this evolution was viewed as a loss of competitiveness explained by the increase of wages or by the fall in productivity (reflected in the evolution of the unit labor cost indicator, ULC), and thereby justifying a process of internal devaluation as the one that led to the labor reforms we will analyze in Chapter 4.

However, different studies have questioned this argument due to the invalidity of the ULC as an aggregated indicator and measure of competitiveness (Felipe y Kumar, 2011; Myant et al., 2016), along with the existence of other factors of greater incidence and empirical observation of the maintenance of share in the world market in the pre-crisis period. Reviewing each of these arguments goes beyond the scope of this chapter, but the analysis presented brings new elements to the debate. In particular, and without denying the importance of price in competition, we consider that analysis of the deficit cannot be isolated from analysis of the specific productive and export specialization of each country.[12]

From the outbreak of the crisis, once the bubble burst, Spain began a progressive reduction of external imbalances, even generating a current account surplus after 2012. This correction is again basically explained by what occurred in trade of goods, the deficit correction of which was highly favored by the consequent reduction of imports (as analyzed in the next chapter), in addition to the slight correction in the rents account and growth in the services surplus. These changes in trade terms are reflected on the financial side by the reduction of debt flows, as one manifestation of a balance sheet recession, as shown in the next chapter.

Considering these arguments, we now analyze the external insertion pattern of the Spanish economy in order to determine, from a trade perspective, whether it displays features of peripheral insertion; subsequently, we analyze what factors may explain the correction of the external balance. As we shall see throughout the chapter, this correction was not due to a basic change in the pattern of specialization, but to cyclical factors that do not modify the structural characteristics of deficit generation. We will identify these characteristics in the pre- and post-crisis periods, highlighting the key sectors in the trade structure, the degree of regional integration, and energy dependence. Particular attention will be given to relevant trade with the EU, comparing this with exchanges outside the EU to assess whether they reinforce the same trend or show different characteristics.

General trends

The Spanish economy has registered gradual increases in its degree of external openness since the 1990s, when the weight of trade over GDP was at 35%; by 2015, that had risen to over 47%. Export and import flows have followed different trends depending on the period considered, thus determining varied evolution of the balance generated.

Between 1995 and 2007, exports grew steadily, but not enough to cover the increase of imports (Figure 2.4). Since the crisis, exports have grown moderately while imports have slowed down. Between 2000 and 2007 (a period of accelerated deficit growth) exports grew at an average rate of 6%, the same rate as between 2011 and 2015,[13] whereas import growth reached 9% in the former period and 2.8% in the latter.[14] Nevertheless, the Spanish economy has been able to maintain relative stability in its global export share (between 1.6% and 1.8%) in a boom period for new exporters worldwide and despite a generalized loss of quota by European countries, except for Germany. As we will see, this is further distinguishable according to the sector considered.

This trend was also evident in services, whose import rates exceeded those of exports between 1999 and 2007. Since the crisis, exports of services have been boosted by, among other factors, a boom in tourism, whereas imports (especially those linked to domestic production activity) have halted, generating positive contributions in financial services and other business services.[15]

The EU is the main customer and supplier for the Spanish economy. In 2015, 66% of exports and 69% of imports were exchanged with EU economies. Nevertheless, these numbers have changed significantly. On the one hand, the deepening of the process of globalization in recent decades has increased exchanges with other regions of the world. On the other hand, as a result of the crisis and the reduction in European demand, exchanges with the EU have been reduced. In 2007, the EU accounted for 71% of Spain's exports and 76% of imports.

Until 2007, EU and non-EU trade evolved in a similar way (a gradual growth in exports and strong growth in imports, particularly after 2004), but trends have changed since the crisis. In exchanges within the EU, imports fell sharply with the crisis and grew very moderately thereafter, whereas exports maintained slight but steady growth, partially correcting the traditional trade deficit. In terms of non-EU exchanges, there has been no change in the sign of the trade balance, but the deficit has been reduced since 2010, due to a contraction of imports (highly influenced by the evolution of international energy prices) and a maintenance of export dynamism.[16]

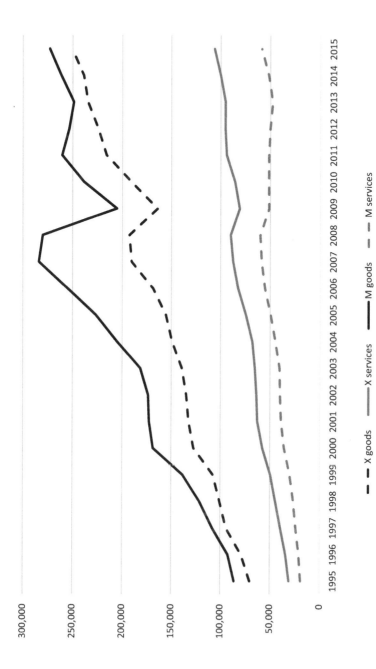

Figure 2.4 Exports and imports of goods and services, 1995–2015 (millions of euro)

Source: Own elaboration with data from Eurostat.

The behavior of trade flows gives us a glimpse at the correction factors at play in the total external position, and these seem to be more related to a reduction of internal activity than to a structural change in trade specialization. In this sense, the policy of internal devaluation would have brought influence as a way of contracting domestic demand and reducing imports, a classic mechanism of stabilization plans that also transpired in Latin America (Álvarez et al., 2009). However, to confirm this, we need to analyze the sectoral composition of exports and imports.

Sectoral composition

Given the foreign-energy dependence of the Spanish economy, it is also important to distinguish trade in energy goods from those of the primary and manufacturing sectors. And within the manufacturing sector, a disaggregated analysis must be carried out in sectoral and technological terms and in the types of goods exchanged according to their final use (input, capital, or consumption goods) in order to assess the external insertion of a given country in a context of manufacturing processes that are increasingly fragmented and articulated along transnational production chains. This cross-analysis will help us to assess whether the recent correction of the trade deficit responds to an improvement in external trade insertion or whether, to the contrary, peripheral patterns have been strengthened.

Excluding trade in energy products (a sector heavily affected by variations in international prices, significantly reduced in recent years), the diagnosis of non-EU trade qualitatively changes. First, given the foreign-energy dependence of the Spanish economy, the weight of imports from outside the EU was reduced from 42% to 25%. As a result, the extra-EU deficit fell significantly after the crisis, and since 2012 a surplus has been generated (Figure 2.5).

However, on the intra-EU side we find the opposite scenario when discounting the energy sector: exports are reduced. This behavior responds to the role of refining petrol destined for the EU. Thus, the energy sector plays a different role depending on the destination and geographical origin of the exchanges.

Non-energy trade data basically underline the importance of trade in goods within the EU (excluding services and energy goods), highlighting the need to particularize the analysis in the main sectors most affected by fragmentation processes at the regional dimension.

If we disaggregate trade trends by sectors, we find that most exchanges are concentrated into three manufacturing sectors: automobiles, mechanical machinery, and electrical machinery (similarly to other European economies such as Germany, France, and Italy). However, whereas Germany strengthened the aggregated surplus of these three sectors, Spain generated deficits in them. The same occurred in France as in Spain, whereas Italy achieved positive balances in mechanical machinery, compensating for the deficits of the other two sectors.

These differences respond to the fact that concordances in the export pattern of these economies have occurred only at an aggregate level of the branch, but are sharply differentiated when considering more disaggregated levels within the

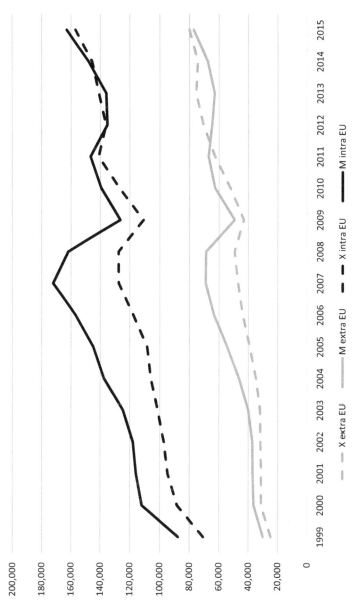

Figure 2.5 Intra-EU and extra-EU trade of goods (excluding energy), 1999–2015 (millions of euro)

Source: Own elaboration with data from Eurostat.

branch, as by type of activity or product, illuminating relative differences among these economies and, fundamentally, at the regional European level.

Given its sectoral specialization (see Table 2.5), the leading role of the automotive sector is highlighted (18% of total exports in 2015 corresponded to vehicles and parts of them destined for the EU), although with a gradual reduction of its weight on exports. Machinery, pharmacy, and those sectors linked with chemical brands are also relevant, being the sectors with greater foreign capital participation, as mentioned in the previous section. Likewise, the evolution of the textile industry,[17] and particularly exports of clothing (which have grown to almost 3% of total exports), is also remarkable.

In fact, the sectoral decomposition of trade changes the previous healthful diagnosis around the maintenance of Spain's market share over total exports. If we focus on the evolution of market shares by product groups,[18] we find that the market share gain between 1999 and 2015 was gathered into certain primary products: meat (growing by more than 5 percentage points), oils and fats (by 2.8 points), textiles (clothing, by more than 4 points), and chemical industry (medicines and perfumes, by more than 1 point). These products share a common characteristic: all of them registered continuous growth in extra-EU exports, to the point of overtaking those exports destined for the EU.

Meanwhile, losses of shares were registered in other primary products: fruits and vegetables (falling by almost 6 points), footwear (by almost 2 points), and automotive (by more than 2 points); and these exports were specifically more oriented to the EU market.

On the import structure, the leading players are again the same sectors (automobiles, mechanical machinery, and electrical machinery), but the primary sectors suffer. In consequence, exchanges with the EU have contributed positively to the total trade balance in primary sectors (mainly, fruit, vegetables, and meat)[19] but negatively (and strongly so) in sectors of machinery and, traditionally, automotive production; however, a change of sign in contribution has been observed in the latter sector since the crisis, and it is now a surplus generator.

The primary sector, with a weight of 15.9% on exports in 2015, and mainly with destination to the EU,[20] remains one of the main positive contributors to the trade balance, which is a traditional feature of peripheral external insertion in its original conception (inter-sectoral). This feature has been strengthened in the post-crisis period, the sector becoming the main source of positive contribution to the trade balance, mainly in its exchanges with the EU.

In any case, the generation of deficits or surpluses should not be considered the ultimate argument to characterize external insertion as being central or peripheral, because the trade balance is determined not only by the trade pattern of each economy, but also by factors of demand.

Thus, in the case of the Spanish economy, the generation of deficits in manufacturing sectors such as vehicles, electrical machinery, or mechanical machinery may be also a symptom of peripheral insertion, if we consider the specific position occupied in productive chains articulated at the regional dimension, along with a structural import dependence on inputs, which sharply increased with the growth of domestic demand.[21]

Table 2.5 Main sectors in trade structure and contribution to trade balance, 1999–2015 (weight over totals in %)

Sectors	Exports					
	Weight over total exports			% destinated to EU-27		
	1999	2007	2015	1999	2007	2015
87 Vehicles	24.5	21.0	18.0	90.0	85.7	79.9
84 Machinery	9.7	8.4	7.9	67.7	61.9	53.9
27 Fuels	2.6	5.5	6.6	53.3	31.5	46.6
85 Electrical machinery	6.9	6.6	5.7	69.4	69.8	60.0
30 Pharmaceutical products	1.4	3.6	4.1	81.7	66.1	49.9
39 Plastics	3.1	3.8	3.9	74.3	74.4	68.0
08 Fruits	3.1	2.6	3.3	92.0	90.8	90.8

	Imports					
	Weight over total imports			% originated in EU-27		
	1999	2007	2015	1999	2007	2015
27 Fuels	7.1	14.9	13.4	12.2	16.2	16.2
87 Vehicles	18.3	15.2	12.9	89.2	85.9	86.2
84 Machinery	13.5	11.1	9.7	79.1	82.3	77.4
85 Electrical machinery	9.4	9.2	8.0	78.6	68.9	65.0
30 Pharmaceutical products	2.2	3.0	4.9	77.7	77.7	74.5
39 Plastics	3.2	3.1	3.6	86.7	83.7	78.7
29 Organic chemicals	2.7	2.6	3.1	70.2	60.8	55.5

	Contribution to trade balance					
	Negative contributions, weight over total			Balance with EU, negative contributions, weight over total		
	1999	2007	2015	1999	2007	2015
27 Fuels	−22.3	−32.7	−86.3	4.0	−11.4	8.5
85 Electrical machinery	−17.9	−10.5	−32.4	−90.6	−91.4	−74.4
84 Machinery	−26.5	−15.2	−29.2	−93.4	−109.6	−145.2
29 Organic chemicals	−5.3	−3.4	−19.2	−89.0	−44.4	−49.8
	Positive contributions, weight over total			Balance with EU, positive contributions, weight over total		
02 Meat	1.1	1.1	14.4	100.8	83.1	66.9
07 Vegetables	6.1	2.7	19.0	111.0	114.5	102.9
08 Fruits	8.2	3.4	24.5	108.6	111.8	115.6
87 Vehicles	2.7	−3.4	41.3	116.2	−107.6	57.1

Notes: Contributions to trade balance are calculated using absolute values in order to keep the real contribution of each sector; the sign of a negative contribution is thus not cancelled by the total trade deficit.

Source: Own elaboration with data from Eurostat.

Thus, with trade structures apparently very similar to its neighboring countries, Spain has generated trade deficits while obtaining surpluses mainly in the primary sectors. However, as was pointed out in the introduction, it is necessary to overcome the traditional inter-sectoral diagnosis of peripheral insertion, especially when comparing countries with similar structures, as in Europe; instead, the trade pattern analysis should be conducted from an intra-sectorial approach while taking into account the growing fragmentation and internationalization of the production process.

The importance of trade in intermediate inputs shows the high degree of international production fragmentation, with processes articulated through trade flows where external positions are hierarchized according to their specialization in the transnationalized production process. But despite its significance in the trade structure, the exchange of industrial inputs maintains its traditional negative contribution to the trade balance of the Spanish economy. This diagnosis can be further extended to the segments of capital and final goods, in that the generation of surplus has concentrated almost exclusively on the primary sector and on exports of vehicles.

Moreover, the degree of regionalization of manufacturing production processes is accentuated if we consider that, by 2015, more than 74% of imports of capital goods and 63% of industrial inputs originated within the EU.[22]

Therefore, the Spanish structural deficit responds to three related characteristics: the scarcity of export productive tissue, the lower position of segments in sectors articulated within the EU and, in consequence, the import dependency of industrial inputs (reactivated by growth of domestic demand).

From a dynamic perspective, internal productive deficiencies generate import needs for industrial inputs and capital goods when production is reactivated, thus relegating the positive contributions to primary sectors. As a result, the capacity to generate added value through an increase in exports is limited, given the import dependence on inputs and the specific segment in the chain, to which might be added the scarce linkages within the Spanish economy between manufacturing and services.

Technological differentiation of the trade structure

The deficiencies noted in the sectoral analysis are even more evident in terms of the technological content of trade. The Spanish economy has registered an export concentration in medium-technology and primary goods, whereas the share of high-technology exports has remained stable since the crisis (Table 2.6).

On the import side, a high concentration in technology is again evident, although this has lost weight to the energy sector since the end of the crisis. High-tech imports remain a deficit-generating category, in contrast to primary goods. As already mentioned, with the crisis there was some correction in the goods balance, and from a technological perspective, that correction has been due to medium-technology and primary goods and to manufacturing related to the energy sector.

Table 2.6 Export and import structure by technological content, 1999–2015 (%)

	1999	2007	2015
	Exports		
High technology	8.7	10.8	10.6
Medium technology	44.8	41.7	37.3
Low technology	15.5	15.3	16.1
Primary	26.3	25.8	27.6
Energy	2.3	4.6	4.7
Unclassified	2.4	2.0	3.8
	Imports		
High technology	13.8	13.9	14.4
Medium technology	41.7	35.5	32.9
Low technology	14.4	14.8	16.8
Primary	22.3	19.9	21.8
Energy	6.7	15.0	13.1
Unclassified	1.1	0.8	1.0

Note: We used the OECD criterion on Eurostat data for the technological content distinction, for which the conversion of the SITC (rev.3) classification to the Harmonized System (HS07) has been necessary in order to maintain the technological distinction according to the OECD criteria and to distinguish between extra- and intra-EU exchanges.

Source: Own elaboration with data from Eurostat.

However, this can be nuanced by distinguishing exchanges with the EU from those with the rest of the world. Looking exclusively at intra-EU trade according to technological content (Figure 2.6), we find that import dependency persists in high technology, whereas the generation of surplus has been relegated almost exclusively to primary goods.

The technological differentiation of trade shows maintenance of the traditional features of exchanges within the EU, which represent most of Spain's trade. The primary sector has maintained its positive contribution to the trade balance, and the medium-value segments have been strengthened, keeping dependence on segments with higher technological content.

Therefore, the process of integration and regional productive articulation appears to have resulted in a worsening of the structural position of the Spanish economy, and this has not been corrected since the outbreak of the crisis.

This does not prevent an aggregate correction of the trade balance, which conceals different sectorial patterns, particularly those more affected by productive fragmentation. Likewise, it should be borne in mind that a trade balance is determined by its export pattern, as a reflection of internal productive capacities, but also by the evolution of imports, linked also to domestic demand.

The specific way in which the trade balance is determined, and how it has been adjusted following the crisis, is indicative of the greater or lesser peripheral condition of an economy. In the case of Spain, the automobile sector is especially

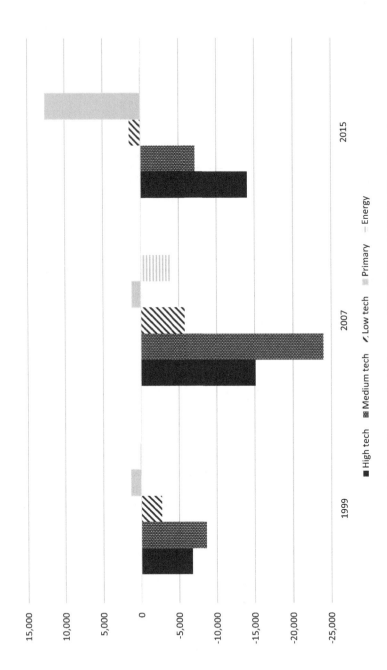

Figure 2.6 Contributions to trade balance by technological content, 1999, 2007, and 2015 (millions of euro)

Source: Own elaboration with data from Eurostat.

illustrative. First, this is the most relevant manufacturing sector in terms of both exports and imports. Second, the sector has improved, from increasing its deficit contribution to trade balance, to becoming the main positive contribution. Third, it has maintained high interdependence with EU partners in a sector where production is organized along regional chains with a high degree of fragmentation so that aggregate flows at the national-sectoral level hide various segments of specialization.

However, the Spanish automobile sector has progressively lost world market share due to the shift of productive capacities to Eastern Europe. This is closely related to a pattern of intra-sectoral specialization characterized mainly by a high share of final goods (namely, low- and medium-range cars), maintaining a strong import dependency on parts and components despite the relative dynamism of this subsector in Spain.

In fact, the generation of positive contributions to trade balances by vehicles can be seen to run parallel to a deficit of parts and components. More precisely, if we take into account the specialization of the Spanish subsector of automotive parts and components and compare it with its requirements for input, the Spanish automotive industry is specialized in parts and components of medium and low value, maintaining a high import dependence on components of higher added value (engines, transmissions, and braking systems).

Both these issues explain the worsening of the trade balance for the automotive industry concurrent with an increase in domestic demand in a sector where the participation of foreign capital is particularly relevant, as mentioned earlier. In the case of the Spanish economy, the main manufacturing sectors in its trade structure have been those with the largest shares of foreign capital, as well as those whose production processes are more fragmented and regionally articulated. Therefore, in a period of significant growth of domestic demand (as in 1995–2007), and despite a relative importance of a high range of vehicles, the export pattern remains unchanged along with the position occupied within the chain, thus generating deficits in what has traditionally been a surplus sector.

Evaluating the strategy of internal devaluation, the automotive sector may seem a success: the balance is corrected because the contraction in demand causes a fall in imports of final goods and, in turn, wage adjustment helps to boost exports.[23] However, this success is questioned if we take into account that, using International Monetary Fund terminology, this correction of the balance responds only to the 'stabilization' of the conjuncture without structural changes or changes of position in the chain or in the export pattern. In fact, none of the key sectors in the external dynamics, whether in the productive realm or in the trade structure, led the growth dynamics in the growth period (as shown in Chapter 1), which indicates that the external insertion has not been key in the growth model, and the growth period did not contribute to transforming Spain's peripheral external insertion.

This is probably one of the clearest signs of the country's weak articulation in regional chains and its strong reliance on foreign capital in terms of geographical location of activities. The divergences between the external insertion patterns of central and peripheral European economies is strongly determined by the variable articulation of national export sectors in both global and regional production chains led by TNCs. And this scenario has not changed following the crisis.

Conclusions

In this chapter, we have assumed the validity of the C-P approach and its usefulness in two senses: i) it allows for understanding the hierarchical character of international economic relations, from which it is possible to evaluate the extent of changes to external insertion patterns; and ii) it provides valuable elements for linking this external insertion with internal factors in the explanation of the economic dynamics of a given country.

Based on these approaches, as we have shown, the trade and productive insertion of the Spanish economy is hampered by the limitations of its productive model, as seen in Chapter 1. We have observed the importance of phenomena such as the role of intra-industry trade or the importance of FDI flows in the services sector associated with processes of capital centralization. However, this dynamic, much as in other European countries, contains a modality of insertion that maintains significant weaknesses that the literature associates with dependent or peripheral insertion.

This profile of insertion has promoted and been simultaneously strengthened by a dynamic of strong external debt related to the real estate bubble and made possible by European monetary integration, which will be analyzed in the next chapter. On the one hand, the presence of foreign capital has been accentuated in the main manufacturing branches and in those of higher technological intensity, without registering a transformation of the export structure of the Spanish economy. These are precisely the sectors most integrated in transnational chains and those that have experienced a process of production fragmentation and articulation, as characterized by the presence of large transnational groups, where power over and control of productive relations are directly related to the segment of the chain in which the economy is specialized.

This sectoral concentration in the trade structure is similar to that of other European countries, which would suggest the importance of the regional geographical dimension in the articulation of these fragmented sectors and the different segments of the chain. In fact, the sectoral breakdown of the trade analysis changes the positive diagnosis regarding Spain's maintenance of world market share during the pre-crisis period, where gains have been concentrated among extra-EU partners, whereas trade with the EU, Spain's main customer and supplier, continues to feature import dependency for inputs and technology and the generation of surplus is relegated to primary sectors and the automotive sector. Also, an export specialization in lower technological content, contrary to its import pattern, has implications in terms of contributions to trade balances, as well as consequences (perhaps more relevant) in the spheres of productivity and income distribution.

The weaknesses of the insertion pattern in Spain are also evident from a perspective of international production control, where despite a very significant increase in FDI outflows, insertion continues to be dependent on foreign capital, particularly in those sectors with the highest technological content. Moreover, this is manifested in some of the most relevant sectors in terms of exports, thus reducing potential toward an export-growth strategy and increasing the degree of dependence on corporate strategies and production decisions by large TNCs.

The strong geographical concentration of exchanges within the EU, upon whose demand Spain depends more heavily than elsewhere, must also be remarked. The growth of non-EU exports, which has been notable after the crisis, has not been large enough to balance the importance of intra-EU trade, particularly in those sectors most affected by organization and specialization within regional chains.

The outbreak of the crisis affected certain elements of Spanish external insertion, but behind an apparently positive evolution was hidden a deepening of earlier dynamics rather than a significant change to the main features of Spain's external insertion. From a trade perspective, the change in the current account balance has resulted from a significant contraction of imports and a deepening of the export specialization pattern in relative terms, in the export of services, and in the manufacturing sectors more inserted into regional production chains. In addition, the export pattern has shown low diversification in sectoral and technological terms, mainly concentrated into three manufacturing sectors and primary goods. Excluding the energy sector, the main manufacturing branches both in exports and imports are characterized by high production fragmentation at the regional dimension. As a result, most exchanges of goods remained concentrated within the EU space, where Spain has accentuated the structural weakness of its trade insertion profile, particularly in terms of its dependence on imports of inputs, capital goods, and technology.

Therefore, the Spanish structural deficit responds to three related characteristics: the scarcity of export productive tissue, the position occupied in lower segments of sectors articulated within the EU, and, in consequence, the import dependency on industrial inputs (reactivated by growth of domestic demand).

Domestic production deficiencies generate the need to import both industrial inputs and capital goods when a production process is reactivated, thus limiting export growth strategies that increase added value. The generation of current account deficits in periods of growth and the nature of their subsequent correction confirm the existence of a dependent external insertion pattern, both from the perspective of inter-sectoral insertion (surplus contributions to trade balances of primary sectors, deficits in machinery) and intra-sectoral insertion (importance of machinery sectors in exports and imports) with negative contributions to trade balance.

Finally, it should be noted that the internal devaluation strategy has shown results in key sectors of Spain's export pattern, such as transport equipment (which increased its participation in the export structure), as well as in the contraction of imports. Thus, the economy has not altered the main features of its external insertion pattern; rather, it has deepened those features, as revealed by the high dependence on importation of inputs and by the control of production process by foreign capital. Meanwhile, the devaluation strategy has had perverse effects both on labor relations and the income distribution pattern in the Spanish economy, as will be discussed in Chapters 4 and 5.

Notes

1 Author names are given in alphabetical order, as both share equal responsibility for this chapter.
2 This literature inspired many critics, both mainstream and Marxist. However, different authors have argued for the validity of many of their arguments (Di Filippo, 1998; Fisher, 2015).
3 Although the C-P approach fundamentally derived from analysis of external insertion, in the original approach the articulation between the two facets was part of a general theory of economic dynamic which included all areas of economic activity (Pérez and Vernengo, 2012). Analyzing the asymmetries generated around the distribution of the productivity gains generated from technical progress allows for the linking of production and distribution, as discussed in the Introduction. Given the focus on external insertion, this chapter does not address a full analysis of these elements but their connection underlies the chapters of this book.
4 Analyzing the full extent of a C-P approach requires the consideration of other aspects such as duality in structures of production or convergence in productivity and wages. These issues go beyond the scope of this chapter.
5 Two national sources provide FDI data: The Bank of Spain (the Central Bank), through the balance of payments, and the Ministry of Economy, through its Investment Registry (Datainvex). In this chapter, we generally employ the second source because it allows for easier differentiation between gross and net investments (divestments being included in the first but not in the second) and because it allows a discounting of the flows associated with holding operations through ETVEs. For international comparisons, the source used is UNCTAD, which in turn uses Central Bank statistics; hence the data provided by this source are superior in value to the net FDI flows with which we work. As an example of the difference between gross and net inflows, with and without ETVEs, in 2004, gross inflows of FDI amounted to more than €19 billion, whereas net inflows without ETVE operations were €799 million.
6 Especially from the EU-15, the main investor.
7 Until the end of the 1990s, FDI outflows were very concentrated in Latin America, but since 2000, investment in the EU (currently the main recipient of Spanish FDI) has gained importance. However, the European role is greater as an investor than as a recipient, showing that Spanish FDI has a different position in relation to the EU and Latin America.
8 Datainvex only provides data on the FDI stock for the period 2007–2014. The source used for the activities of foreign affiliates is the FILINT database of the Spanish National Institute of Statistics (in Spanish, INE), which also presents data for the post-crisis period (2008–2013). This limits our analysis by not allowing us to establish a comparison with previous years.
9 Producer-driven indicator: $P_j^P = \sum_{i=1}^n log\,(X_{ji}/Y_i + 1)$, where X_{ji} are exports from country j to country i, and Y_i is total imports from country i (Mahutga, 2013).
10 Buyer-driven indicator: $P_j^B = \sum_{i=1}^n log\,(Y_{ij}/X_i + 1)$, where Y_{ij} are imports to country j from country i, and X_i is total exports of country i (Mahutga, 2013).
11 Measured in euros, this was the largest deficit in the EU, and the third in terms of GDP behind Greece and Portugal, which followed a shared pattern (the usual justification for their categorization as Mediterranean periphery economies, given their growing need for external financing).
12 In the structuralist center–periphery analysis, chronic deficits in the current account were linked to the weakness of the productive structure, emphasizing that a peripheral

insertion tended to generate lower growth of exports than of imports due to the associated different income elasticity of each trade structure.

13 Excluding 2009 and 2010, given the strong variation resulting from the crisis and the consequent data distortion. In 2009, exports fell sharply compared to the previous year (−14.8%) to rebound in 2010 with exceptional growth (+17.7%).

14 Excluding 2009 and 2010, where imports decreased by 26.5% with a subsequent rebound of 17.3%.

15 Between 1999 and 2007, the average variation in exports and imports of services was at 7% and 10%, respectively; between 2008 and 2015, exports grew by 3%, whereas imports stagnated (up only 0.2%).

16 Exports to non-EU countries went from 26% of total trade in 1999 to 35% in 2015. The United States is the main non-European partner (in 6th place, with 4.5% of total trade in 2015), followed by Morocco (9th place, 2.4%), Turkey (10th place, 2.0%), and China (12th place, 1.7%).

17 Within the textile industry we can find tissue exports, which have lost weight on the export structure, and clothing exports, which have gained importance. On the other hand, the footwear industry regained weight in exports after having lost it in recent decades.

18 Data according to UNCTAD, SITC rev. 3 with three digits of disaggregation and considering those goods that change world market share by more than one percentage point and represented more than 1% of Spanish exports in 2015.

19 Items 0, 1, and 20–26 according to the Harmonized System classification; both raw and unprocessed raw materials, including the processed food industry, tobacco and beverages.

20 Significantly influenced by the development of the Common Agricultural Policy (CAP).

21 An economy can occupy a peripheral productive position and still generate trade surpluses. This is the case with several economies in Eastern Europe, which have registered industrialization processes in sectors with a high degree of external orientation, but low growth of the domestic market, thereby not increasing imports.

22 In the case of exports figures are lower, 53% and 57%, respectively.

23 Although this might be nuanced by distinguishing between final vehicles and parts and components. Between 1995 and 2007, Spain lost 1.7 points of share in final vehicles and gained 0.7 points in parts and components; since the outbreak of the crisis, Spain has increased its market share of finished vehicles by 0.2 points and decreased in parts and components by 0.8 points.

References

Álvarez, I., Luengo, F. and Uxó, J. (2013): *Fracturas y crisis en Europa*, Madrid: Clave Intelectual.

Álvarez, M.E. and Fernández-Otheo, C.M. (2015): 'El capital extranjero y la exportación española', in R. Myro (dir.), *España en la inversión directa internacional*, Madrid: Instituto de Estudios Económicos, pp. 203–242.

Álvarez, N., Buendía, L., Mateo, J.P., Medialdea, B., Molero, R., Montanyà, M., Paz, M.J. and Sanabria, A. (2009): *Ajuste y salario. Las consecuencias del neoliberalismo en América Latina y Estados Unidos*, Madrid: Fondo de Cultura Económica.

Chase-Dunn, C. and Rubinson, R. (1977): 'Toward a Structural Perspective on the World-System', *Politics and Society*, 7 (4), pp. 453–476.

Di Filippo, A. (1998): 'La visión centro-periferia hoy', in *Revista de la CEPAL, Número Extraordinario, 'CEPAL cincuenta años, reflexiones sobre América Latina y el Caribe'*, CEPAL, pp. 175–186.

Evans, P. (1979): 'Beyond Center and Periphery: A Comment on the Contribution of the World System Approach to the Study of Development', *Sociological Inquiry*, 49(4), pp. 15–20.

Felipe, J. and Kumar, U. (2011): 'Unit Labor Costs in the Eurozone: The Competitiveness Debate Again', *Working Paper (Levy Economics Institute)*, 651.

Fernández-Otheo, C.M. and Myro, R. (2015): 'La inversión exterior directa de España. Una perspectiva agregada y comparada', in R. Myro (dir.), *España en la inversión directa internacional*, Madrid: Instituto de Estudios Económicos, pp. 25–122.

Fisher, A.M. (2015): 'The End of Peripheries? On the Enduring Relevance of Structuralism for Understanding Contemporary Global Development', *Development and Change*, 46 (4), pp. 700–732.

Fitoussi, J.P. (2010): 'Politiques macroeconomiques et reformes structurelles: Bilan et perspectives de la gouvernance economique de l'Union Europeenne', *Document de travail (Observatoire Français des Conjonctures Économiques)*, 2010–07.

García, A., Morillas, A. and Ramos, C. (2007): 'Núcleos productivos en Europa y España. Un estudio a partir de modelos discretos centro-periferia', *Estudios de Economía Aplicada*, 25 (1), pp. 485–510.

Gereffi, G., Humphrey, J. and Sturgeon, T. (2005): 'The Governance of Global Value Chains', *Review of International Political Economy*, 12 (1), pp. 78–104.

Guillén, M.F. and García-Canal, E. (2011): *Las nuevas multinacionales. Las empresas españolas en el mundo*, Barcelona: Ariel.

Hopkins, T.K. and Wallerstein, I. (1977): 'Patterns of Development of the Modern World-System', *Review (Fernand Braudel Center)*, 1 (2), pp. 111–145.

Lapavitsas, C., Kaltenbrunner, A., Lambrinidis, G., Lindo, D., Meadway, J., Michell, J., Painceira, J.P., Pires, E., Powell, J., Stenfors, A. and Teles, N. (2010): *The Eurozone Between Austerity and Default*, London: Research on Money and Finance.

Mahutga, M.C. (2013): 'Global Models of Network Organization: The Positional Power of Nations and Economic Development', *Review of International Political Economy*, 21 (1), pp. 157–194.

Martínez Peinado, J. (2011): 'La estructura teórica centro/periferia y el análisis del sistema económico global: ¿obsoleta o necesaria?', *Revista de Economía Mundial*, 29, pp. 27–57.

Myant, M., Theodoropoulou, S. and Piasna, A. (eds.). (2016): *Unemployment, Internal Devaluation and Labour Market Deregulation in Europe*, Brussels: ETUI.

Pérez, E. and Vernengo, M. (2012): '¿Una pareja dispareja? Prebisch, Keynes y la dinámica capitalista', *Estudios Críticos del Desarrollo*, 2 (3), pp. 158–193.

Solaz, M. (2016): 'Cadenas globales de valor y generación de valor añadido: el caso de la economía española', *WP-EC (IVIE)*, 2016–01.

United Nations Conference on Trade and Development (UNCTAD) (2012): *World Investmen Report*, Geneva: UNCTAD.

3 The Spanish financial sector

Debt crisis and bailout

Eduardo Garzón Espinosa, Bibiana Medialdea García, and Antonio Sanabria Martín[1]

Introduction

Following analysis of the fundamentals of the Spanish economy's growth model and external insertion, this chapter examines the financial dynamics on which both have been sustained. This dynamic began with a process of overindebtedness in which expansion of the economy was rooted; this process created a high degree of financial vulnerability, caused by the outbreak of a private debt crisis that dragged the economy as a whole into recession. In this chapter, we also examine how this debt crisis and its implications have been managed. As we shall see, the imbalances that accrued in the financial sector of the economy during the expansionary period were the most obvious manifestation (consequence and cause) of the limits faced by the Spanish economy in terms of accumulation (as analyzed in Chapter 1), accentuated by the dependent nature of Spain's external productive and commercial insertion (as explained in Chapter 2).

The study presented here is based on an analytical approach launched from two basic ideas. The first refers to the intrinsically cyclical nature of capitalist economies and the decisive role of demand (especially investment) within the cycle (Keynes, 1936; Kalecki, 1971; Palazuelos and Fernandez, 2007). The second insists on the centrality of the financial dimension in macroeconomic dynamics, from a perspective known as the endogenous money approach. This assumes a close link between the autonomous creation of money (debt) by the financial system and the economy's demand (Moore, 1988; Wray, 1990; Keen, 2011).

Keen's views on the role of private debt in the business cycle are particularly useful for our study. According to his perspective, in a monetary economy, economic growth is driven by aggregate demand, which is in turn financed (at least partially) through credit. This volume of credit is determined by expectations of profit, which, when promising, will encourage credit expansion. That is, the volume of credit is determined by future profit expectations, not by results obtained in the past. The important thing here is that banks, through credit, create additional purchasing power that allows finance to meet demand. Therefore, aggregate demand should be equal to GDP plus debt variation (Keen, 2011: 339). Debt does have effects on aggregate demand, contrary to neoclassical postulates. Thus, credit creation is not a problem if it does not stray far from nominal GDP growth.

In that case, financial obligations are transformed over time into production of goods and services so that sales will allow for the settling of accounts and the assumption of new debt commitments. If this does not happen (if credit expansion is detached from GDP variation), problems emerge.

The existence and consequences of such a divergence between the level of debt and the real generation of income are well explained by Minsky in his hypothesis of financial instability. In a schematic way, Minsky (1992) poses three possible relationships between debt and economic agents. In a first phase, the economic agents are covered and can meet their commitments through the income generated by their activities. The maintenance over time of such an expansive phase builds more leverage, which allows for greater potential benefits. To the extent that expectations are met, this will tend to increase indebtedness and to neglect risk. This is a second, speculative phase, in which income derives more and more from new debts. In a third and final phase, called by Minsky the 'Ponzi phase', economic agents can no longer face the payment of principal or interest, so all that remains is to sell assets (to obtain liquidity) or else to borrow more. Meanwhile, economic agents simultaneously attempt to reduce their debt, through what Fisher (1933) called 'debt deflation' (or Koo, 2011, more recently termed 'balance sheet recession').

In the following sections, we develop our analysis of the evolution of Spain's financial system and its links with the general economic dynamics using the analytical schema described earlier. In the second section, we begin by identifying and briefly explaining the basic elements that define and distinguish the Spanish financial system. In the third section, we examine the expansionary stage of the Spanish economy, in which the vulnerability that led to the private debt crisis was born. The fourth section is devoted to analysis of how, through private overindebtedness and from the beginning of the crisis, a dynamic was introduced that dragged the state into fiscal crisis and the economy into severe recession. The fifth section explains the logic behind the debt crisis; specifically, we analyze the subsequent bank bailout and how the process was nothing but a vast socialization of financial losses. Finally, we state our conclusions on issues raised throughout the chapter.

Basic elements of the Spanish financial system

The current structure of the Spanish financial system accumulates changes derived from world financialization (Medialdea and Sanabria, 2013) and the processes of liberalization and European integration, underway since the mid-1980s. These processes led to significant reforms, but two basic features persisted intact: a strong banking sector, and national ownership of the financial entities.

The first of these features is common to other non–Anglo-Saxon European economies, although in Spain the sector is more oriented to retail banking.[2] Bank credit is therefore the main method of financing households, but also companies: more than 90% of business financing comes from bank loans (data from the Bank of Spain [BoS]). Alternative options, such as the issuance of corporate bonds and other securities, remain comparatively scarce.

In terms of the second feature, credit institutions remain largely in Spanish hands. Unlike in other sectors (for example, the automobile industry), the process of internationalization did not involve a change of bank ownership towards foreign capital. This was basically due to the model of the deposit institutions: a retail bank, oriented to retail activity, with an extensive network of branches and territorial rooting in the case of savings banks,[3] represented a barrier to entry despite liberalization.

Another factor (derived from previous banking crises) must be added to this 'natural barrier': the already existing concentration of this activity. In fact, the banking crises of the mid-1970s and early 1990s led to a process of concentration, later strengthened by the grouping and subsequent privatization of public banks between 1993 and 1998.[4] Governments of the time considered that larger entities could better face competition in a context characterized by the liberalization of capital markets and the process of European integration.

The intense territorial expansion of the saving banks, closely linked to the growth of the GDP of each province (Delgado et al., 2008), gave strong competition to the banks. In fact, the deposit market share had been higher for savings banks since the early 1990s, and their credit market share surpassed that of banks in the mid-2000s (Analistas Financieros Internacionales AFI, 2012: 233–234). This factor, coupled with the transnational expansion of some Spanish companies, helped to motivate the international leap of the largest banks, especially Banco Santander and Banco Bilbao Vizcaya Argentaria (BBVA).

The process of financial liberalization and European integration implied important changes in the Spanish financial system.[5] In a gradual way, the financial dimension of the economic growth model was transformed from a model of attracting domestic savings to one more oriented toward external financing, given the greater liquidity offered by the free international movement of capital and financial innovations in the global market. The state obtained financing through the issuance of securities in debt markets, to the detriment of other prior mechanisms, such as mandatory investment ratios in public debt for banks and savings banks, bank loans with regulated interest rates, or the recurrent appeal to the BoS (Vilariño, 2001: 17–24). Likewise, the primary objective of monetary policy (now managed by the Central Bank) became price stability in order to control inflation. To this end, the BoS was given autonomy from 1994 and was prevented from acting as a state banker.[6]

Growth regime financing (1995–2007)

The process of the expansion and subsequent fall of the Spanish economy faithfully followed the model of boom and recession under financial instability as described by Minsky, amplified in this case by access to abundant external financing. In this way, a Spanish credit bubble was formed in the context of the global credit bubble. The new expansionary cycle began with the end of the crisis of the EMS, provoked by the monetary policy of Germany after its reunification. The unilateral rise of their interest rates forced the other participant countries to lift their own rates in order to stop capital flight to Germany and to control exchange rates. The end of the recession of the early 1990s and the reinforcement of irrevocability in the system of fixed exchange rates implied the adoption of a common currency. The Spanish economy began a particularly lengthy expansionary cycle in the latter half of the 1990s. In this section, we analyze the nature of that expansion through the behavior of credit and private debt.

First, before the recession, the Spanish economy exhibited a stable and lasting growth dynamic, which encouraged the expansion of credit to households and companies. According to data from the BoS, the annual growth rate of loans to companies and residential households moved into two digits (10.3%) in the first quarter of 1997, surpassing 20% year-on-year from June 2005.

When credit maintains growth levels significantly higher than the nominal GDP, it implies that part of the debt is spent on financing the acquisition of existing assets (thus having no impact on GDP). Two assets express this speculative bubble with special eloquence: securities quoted on the stock exchange, and the real estate sector. With respect to the former, speculative demand led to the IBEX-35 benchmark index in Spain, which multiplied by 2.5 between 2002 and 2007, to five times higher than the 1995 level, and by 11.4 between 1996 and 2007. Thus, it was not surprising that the ratio between the effective value and the nominal value of securities went from 1.7 in 1996 to 10.5 in 2007, according to data from the Spanish National Institute of Statistics (in Spanish, INE). The huge demand for securities inflated the value of listed companies, which increased their ability to access credit.

But the main bubble and driver of debt demand in Spain was in the real estate sector, in line with the dynamics of the accumulation process analyzed in Chapter 1. According to INE data, between 1999 and 2005, the price per square meter of the non-subsidized market housing increased by 117%.[7] The fact that the resident population between ages 20 and 49 (in principle, the fundamental component of demand for housing) grew at a significantly lower rate in that period (by 27% according to INE data) suggests the existence of a speculative dynamic, where the demand for housing as a good was subordinated to the expectations of obtaining capital gains (Sanabria and Medialdea, 2016).

Another notable speculative symptom manifested in the way appraisal prices grew at higher rates than market sales prices.[8] Demand expectations were such that the total number of building permits in Spain for 2006 exceeded those of France and Italy combined (EMF, 2016). It is therefore evident that such demand growth was largely due to purely speculative factors. The construction of new housing had a positive impact on GDP, thanks to the strong multiplier effect of construction, as analyzed in Chapter 1, but the speculative ends caused credit expansion to be much higher. Figure 3.1 shows the evolution of credit, disaggregated according to several destinations. The special predilection for the sectors related to (though not limited to) construction is evident here.

The Ponzi agent in the case of Spain was precisely in this sector, and more specifically in the real estate developer, whose role is just to promote a building program on a plot over which he has rights and to seek funding, but not build

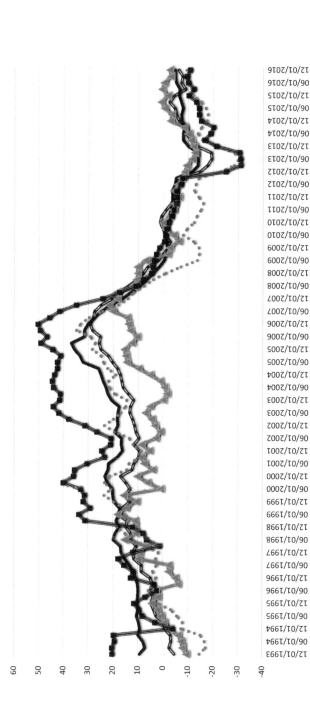

Figure 3.1 Credit by destination, 1993–2016 (annual growth rates)

Source: Own elaboration with data from EoS.

Housing & building activities

Building activities

Production activities

Real estate developer's loan

Industry without building activities

by themselves. The stock of this sort of credit represented in 2008 30% of GDP (€300 billion) according to BoS data. This was off-plan property, without further guarantees, so that when a project failed, the lender was left with undeveloped land and/or unfinished work as the only (illiquid) asset – unsuitable collateral against bad credit.

Finally, as illustrated in Figure 3.2, the novelty of this expansionary cycle did not lie in the intense pace of credit growth itself (as had happened before), but in the volume of demand financed by debt; that is, in the disconnection between credit growth and GDP growth. This was illustrative of the speculative phase of Minsky in its full splendor, but with one particularity: the demand for debt was financed abroad. This amplified the capacity of investment, but also its vulnerability.

Vulnerabilities

The movement to a (private) debt-driven growth model made it intrinsically unstable and vulnerable not only to potential adverse events, but even to a simple slowdown in credit growth. Faced with such a credit boom, and given the predominance of banking in the sector, it is not surprising that the assets of the banking system multiplied by 3.5 between 1997 and 2007 without an equivalent increase in the system's own resources (IFA, 2012: 233).

In order to sustain such growth, the financial entities took advantage of abundant external financing, in what is known as 'leverage in liquidity' (*ibid.*). Thus, an added vulnerability arose because financial institutions increasingly resorted to the external sector through the debt markets, instead of obtaining financing through deposits (their own funds).

Two risks were thus combined: credit risk, increased by a higher level of leverage (tolerated by the BoS as a supervisory body), and increasing reliance on external financing. Not surprisingly, the sharp increase in foreign debt (which since the end of 2014 had already exceeded 100% of GDP in gross terms) continued its rise. It should be added that this risk to external financing was exacerbated by the concentration of credit in the real estate sector, which in the early stages of the crisis exceeded 60% of the total portfolio.

The current account deficit was another expression of strong external dependence (referred to in Chapter 2), which reached 11% of GDP (previously unheard of in the Spanish economy). This implies that investment was much higher than domestic savings so that the gap had to be covered by an uptake in resources from abroad. National savings barely covered 60% of the resource requirements for investment in the phase of greatest imbalance (Jiménez-Ridruejo Ayuso, 2014: 157). Apart from obtaining foreign credit, the main inflow of funds to compensate for the current account deficit was, from 2004, portfolio investment, mainly concentrated in notes and bonds, including mortgage bonds. In 2007, portfolio investment was almost enough to offset the need for external financing, with incomes equivalent to 9% of GDP that year.

This process had at least four implications. First, the large-scale purchase from abroad of marketable securities fueled the bubble of these assets and, along with

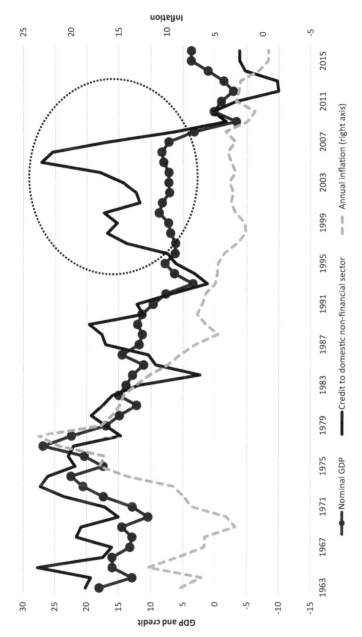

Figure 3.2 Credit to non-financial resident sectors, nominal GDP, and inflation, 1963–2016 (annual growth rates)

Source: Own elaboration with data from BoS, INE, and AMECO.

that, the indebtedness capacity of listed companies as their apparent valuation increased. Second, the boom in the securities market prompted shorter-term business management, more concerned with offering immediate results than the company could revalue, in addition to bonus revenues to management itself. Third, a sudden stop in these portfolio investments would cause a severe correction in prices, aggravated in cases of high corporate indebtedness. And fourth, the fact that the main fundraising came from portfolio investments revealed the weak foundations on which the largest growth cycle in the Spanish economy in recent decades was based.

The bankruptcy of Lehman Brothers and the consequent shortage in international capital markets exploded the credit bubble in the Spanish economy. However, it should be noted that this was not merely a sudden stop, but the consequence of high levels of private indebtedness, now without financing capacity. This was the most obvious manifestation of imbalances in the process of accumulation and of the dependent nature of the external insertion of the Spanish economy, as explained in the previous two chapters.

The euro paradox

A final aspect (in fact linked to external dependence) should be considered: membership in the Eurozone as an added factor of vulnerability. At the onset of the crisis, the Spanish economy discovered that it had borrowed from abroad in a currency that it did not control. The Spanish economy maintained a growth model with external debt expressed in local currency, which had the additional advantage of being a strong currency. Public debt expressed in a local fiduciary currency guarantees its collection, because that debt can always be paid with new monetary issuances. Also, a strong currency means a lower risk for creditors of depreciation in the value of the liability. However, the paradox of the euro is that Spanish debt was issued in a currency that was only nominally local because sovereignty over the issuer (in this case the ECB) was shared with other countries, some of them creditors of the Spanish economy. Thus, the risk of external credit was linked to another risk related to the possible redenomination of its liabilities, which, should that occur, would multiply the total stock of debt (or at least the private debt) as well as the cost of its refinancing. The vulnerability of the economy since the crisis has combined a high level of external debt with the risk of moving from a strong currency to a weak one.

The mere perception by investors of the imminence (real or not) of just such a risk made this a self-fulfilling prophecy, which became real between 2010 and 2012. Capital flight to other places considered safer (like Germany) drained the available liquidity, but this exit of funds did not depreciate the currency, which would have partially mitigated the effects. This made the Spanish economy highly dependent on the ECB and its monetary policy, first because the closure of the interbank market made the ECB the lender of last resort for financial entities to obtain the necessary liquidity to keep up with payment commitments; and second, because only ECB intervention in the secondary market of public debt could avoid the attacks of speculative agents.

The private debt crisis

Origin of the crisis: private overindebtedness

The financial fragility that (as we have explained) the private sector engendered during the growth years was made explicit from September 2008, due to the contagion of the international crisis. Complicated access to external credit and the start of the recession in Spain marked the beginning of a process of financial deleveraging, generalizing the negative impact on credit: the total change in the outstanding amount of credit turned negative for the first time in Spain (and in recorded data).

The cuts in access to external financing placed the business sector (financial and non-financial) in a particularly complicated situation, because their level of overindebtedness was particularly high. In 2007, non-financial corporations accrued debt equivalent to 125% of the country's GDP, and financial-sector companies owed 92.5% of GDP[9] – a large part of this debt had been contracted abroad. Given the impossibility of refinancing such a volume of accumulated liabilities, and in a context adverse to the generation of new income, Spanish companies had serious problems meeting their financial obligations.

The first companies affected were those linked to the real estate and financial sectors, because in addition to being heavily indebted to outside agents, they were directly suffering from the fall in prices stemming from the bursting of the real estate bubble. Other non-financial corporations saw new complications in the refinancing of their high debt volume, so they prioritized the reduction of investments and the destruction of employment, if not their own liquidation and destruction of installed capital: the number of non-financial companies that declared themselves insolvent went from 193 cases in 2004 to 5,721 in 2011 (INE).

On the other hand, as the ECB gradually increased interest rates from 2% in December 2005 to 4.25% in July 2008 (already in recession), the cost of indebtedness for households also increased. Faced with the greater financial cost of high household debt and the strong net destruction of employment, households increased their savings from 5.7% of their disposable income in 2007 to 13.5% in 2009. That process worked to the detriment of consumption, which in 2009 fell to negative growth rates. Lastly, financial institutions drastically reduced credit concessions due to complications in their access to wholesale financing, and because their assets had notably deteriorated thanks to bad loans and new demands by the regulator to increase their capital provisions.

As we shall see at the end of this section, the crisis of private overindebtedness dragged the Spanish economy into a 'recession from over-indebtedness' (Sanabria and Medialdea, 2016): investment decline, job destruction, declines in GDP and in future expectations. But before going into this last aspect, let us first clarify the role of the fiscal crisis in this sequence.

Impact on public accounts

The public accounts were in healthy form at the outbreak of the crisis of overindebtedness. Since Spain's incorporation into the European Economic and Monetary Union

(EMU), the country had always fulfilled the requirements imposed by the Stability Pact. During the years of exorbitant growth and expansion of private debt (1997–2007), the weight of public indebtedness fell dramatically, from 66.2% to 35.5% of GDP. Then the recession triggered a rapid deterioration in the public accounts: between 2007 and 2009, a budgetary surplus of 2% of GDP shifted to a deficit of −11% (Eurostat). This drastic reversal in government finance resulted mainly due to the fall in public revenues and, albeit to a lesser extent, the increase in expenses.

According to Eurostat data, tax revenues fell from 41.7% of GDP in 2007 to 35.2% in 2009. The increase in public spending, in turn, was largely due to automatic activation of public benefits linked to the recessive situation (such as those resulting from the destruction of employment): between 43% and 51% (Lago Peñas, 2012). As we shall see, to this process, the public resources intended to recapitalize banks should be added. In any case, Spanish public spending has always remained below the European average.[10] In short, the impact on public accounts was intensified due to a pro-cyclical tax system and a lower tax burden.

In addition, the paradox of the euro mentioned earlier aggravated this situation. The Spanish state borrows in a currency that it does not control so that the liquidity problems produced as a result of the recession generated a favorable context for speculation and the consequent increase of interest rates. In this environment, a liquidity crisis can lead to solvency problems, not due to the volume of accumulated debt so much as to the conditions for its financing and the spiral that such a dynamic triggers in the face of doubts around ability to pay. This mechanism of increasing interest rates (as a necessary condition for refinancing the debt, simultaneously feeding the need to extend that indebtedness) was not deactivated until July 2012, when the ECB president (at the brink of the solvency crisis) finally declared himself ready to do 'whatever it takes to preserve the euro'.

Although interest rates may be reduced, the increasing volume of debt feeds the total amount of interest to be paid so that the financial problem facing the state goes beyond the rate level. Thus, the burden associated with public debt financing continued to rise to a total cost of 3.5% of GDP in 2014, although its relative weight in GDP has since declined.[11]

In short, far from representing the origin of the crisis, public debt problems arose as a consequence of the recession due to private overindebtedness and its recessive impact on economic activity. Second, the institutional context of the Eurozone imposed a very restrictive framework for managing these initial pressures on public accounts (Sanabria, 2012), restrictions that exacerbated the fiscal crisis. All this, as we will see later, occurred in a context of widespread recession that further damaged the fiscal situation.

Balance sheet recession (2008–2015)

Cuts in the provision of international credit in 2008 were not the origin of the financial shock, but rather a catalyst for more serious problems: evidence of the weaknesses of the prior growth model. In fact, as explained in Chapter 1, several aspects indicated from the very beginning the seriousness of the situation:

investment annual growth became negative in June 2008 (although a change in the cycle had been anticipated since 2006); unemployment had been on the rise for almost a year; and consumption began to decline the last quarter of 2008.

Once access to credit was interrupted, the dynamics of prior growth collapsed, and within a few months the Spanish economy was immersed in a recessive spiral. Such a credit-dependent growth dynamic was fatal to the economy. Business investment, which could not be refinanced as in the past, began to recede, resulting in immediate job destruction and declining production. The consequent drop in income levels depressed consumption and exacerbated the negative impact on demand in a dynamic that fed back and resulted in the recessive spiral that was activated from 2009.

This recession has been particularly serious and difficult to manage due to the context of overindebtedness that originated it (Sanabria and Medialdea, 2016). As in Fisher's study on the Great Depression (1933) and Koo's study of the Japanese crisis (2011), weakness in demand, problems in the financial sector, and overindebtedness of the private sector of the economy made for a particularly dangerous context.

On the one hand, non-financial companies stopped investment due to declining consumption, while at the same time their own problems had to be financed (they prioritized the reduction of indebtedness). Banks, also immersed in their own financial crises and in the context of overindebtedness and general issues of solvency, had no incentive to lend, either to non-financial corporations or to households. Families minimized their consumption due to the demands of unemployment, the greater weight of indebtedness, and/or the increasing propensity to save against future bad prospects. In summary, the behavior of all private-sector agents in this context became a debt minimizer, which Koo characterizes as a 'balance sheet recession'.

Given that exports have obvious limitations as a driving force for demand in an economy such as Spain's (as discussed in Chapter 2), public demand was the only element capable of breaking the recessive spiral. However, in the name of regaining credibility, crisis management opted for the alternative of fiscal austerity. As we will see later, far from addressing the recession and mitigating its effects on the hardest-hit segments of the population, adjustment and austerity policies have served to underpin the economic obstacles to recovery, setting the country on a clear course of regressive socialization of the costs of the crisis.

Adjustment, bailout, and socialization of losses

Adjustment and the priority to regain external confidence

Public bonds in European economies showed very different levels of risk (and profitability) prior to the formation of the EMU, reflecting the dispersion in terms of economic soundness, fiscal consolidation, inflation, and, ultimately, the credibility of the state concerned. However, after the announcement in 1998 that many European countries would share a new single currency, these risk differentials in public bonds were quickly and radically reduced. After all, financial creditors took for granted that the default risk would be practically the same for every economy that joined the EMU. The risk premium of Spain's public bond (the 10-year interest rate differential on the secondary market with respect to the same type of government bond in Germany) remained very stable, around 5 basis points.

However, once the financial shock in U.S. markets began to spread to Europe, the risk premium of some economies (including Spain's) began to increase. Figure 3.3 shows that in 2007, a very volatile growth path commenced, reaching 100 basis points by September 2008 due to the instability and uncertainty sparked by the Lehman Brothers' bankruptcy. Almost two years later, the Greek sovereign debt crisis in May 2010 severely affected the perceived risk of the Spanish public bond in the secondary market, starting a new up-scaling of its spread much more intense than the previous.

At the request of the Council of Economic and Financial Affairs of the European Union, the government reacted – on May 12, 2010, applying significant cuts to many areas of expenditure, with the aforementioned goal of recovering the confidence of international markets. This marked a turning point in the government's economic policy; a brief stage characterized by the implementation of a stimulus plan via public spending was abandoned in order to enter fully into austerity policies aimed at rapidly reducing the public deficit and gaining external competitiveness through internal devaluation (fundamentally based on wage freezes and reductions, as explained in the introductory chapter).[12]

The consecration of the principles of budgetary stability, and the consequent priority of repaying public debt, was made concrete in the constitutional reform of August 2011. Both the Spanish government and European authorities seemed to interpret the crisis as an isolated phenomenon that could be solved by easing the fears of financial creditors.[13]

However, there are compelling reasons to conclude that this was a useless move, even for the purpose it was intended to achieve. This is corroborated by the evolution of Spain's risk premium: at the time of the constitutional reform, it was around 300 basis points, but its rise continued, more than doubling to exceed 600 basis points just a year later. The end of the escalation occurred only on July 27, 2012, thanks to the aforementioned intervention of Mr. Draghi, which assuaged the risk of exit from the euro. Thus, neither austerity policies nor constitutional reform served to reduce the risk premium, but only to reduce coverage of the welfare state, as will be shown in Chapter 5.

Bank bailout

The end of the international credit boom dealt a heavy blow to Spanish banks, increasingly dependent on foreign financing. Spanish banking found itself in an extremely untenable situation due to the new recessive scenario (born of private overindebtedness), overexposure to the building sector, and the poor balance sheets of financial institutions that would usher the collapse of both residential prices and financial assets.

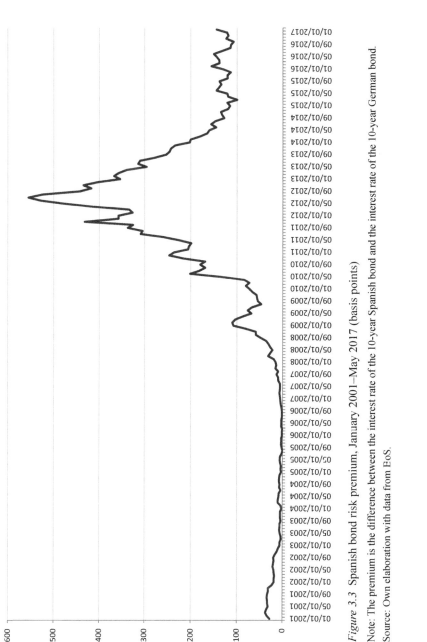

Figure 3.3 Spanish bond risk premium, January 2001–May 2017 (basis points)

Note: The premium is the difference between the interest rate of the 10-year Spanish bond and the interest rate of the 10-year German bond.

Source: Own elaboration with data from EoS.

However, the interpretation of both the Spanish government and European authorities was different: for them, it was merely a problem of credibility. Bank crises were mainly associated with shortfalls in liquidity resulting from the closure of the inter-bank market and wholesale financing markets. The Spanish government's reading of the crisis avoided the overleveraging of banks and their high real estate exposure. These were interpreted as purely exogenous problems in the face of the international financial crisis and the collapse of credit, so the strategy pursued was to provide banks with emergency liquidity while recovering access to finance. And in fact, at the beginning of the crisis, there were reasons to believe that it was not an exaggerated diagnosis.

On the one hand, as a response to the crisis of the 1970s, the BoS had forced the financial entities to make a series of additional provisions known as 'generic' or 'dynamic'. Banks and savings banks set aside reserves of resources additional to those demanded by the risk level of each loan. On the other hand, the mortgage default rate was showing very low levels (around 0.5% of total loans). The likelihood of more extensive mortgage defaults seemed remote: Spanish families do whatever they have to in order not to lose their homes, and also local mortgage legislation is especially favorable to the creditor.

To this we can add three more factors. The first is that, according to data from the Financial Survey of Families of the BoS, almost half of households did not carry any type of debt, which seemed to limit the danger. The second is that banks and savings banks had become the principal real estate agencies in Spain. Thus, despite a drop in residential demand, these entities retained significant real estate assets in their portfolios and could avoid bearish price escalation by putting them up for sale. Finally, the BoS had managed to prevent the banks under its supervision from participating in U.S. derivatives markets, thus eliminating exposure to U.S. 'toxic' assets. Undoubtedly, the BoS' international prestige as a supervisor, already significant, was strongly reinforced.

Unfortunately, time proved that not even these sectoral virtues would be sufficient to compensate for the gaping holes in the balance sheets of banks and savings banks, stemming from the intense concentration of their business in the promotion and construction of real estate assets (tolerated by the regulator). Moreover, the optimistic diagnosis ignored the intense collapse that was to occur in the following years in terms of productive activity, derived from the fall of demand financed through debt.

During the early years of crisis, public aid to local banks was a preventive measure, in contrast to the enormous financial bailouts due to bank restructuring in Germany, the Netherlands, or the United Kingdom. The first of these measures was recourse to the Fund for the Acquisition of Financial Assets: four operations with a value-added €19.3 billion dedicated to the acquisition of quality assets. This was followed by public guarantees on debt issuances by credit institutions, with a limit of up to €100 billion in the so-called Asset Protection Schemes (APS), discussed later. Moreover, there were public guarantees to facilitate the sale of certain failed mergers to other banks. In any case, a public endorsement was granted without clear understanding of the actual situation of the beneficiary entities.

At the same time, the Fund for Orderly Bank Restructuring (or FROB in Spanish) was created in June 2009 to allow the recapitalization of institutions when the deposit guarantee fund proved insufficient and market financing was not available. But the FROB would also later serve to encourage and facilitate (with public money) the process of savings bank mergers.

The gradual revelation of significant difficulties within the different financial institutions emphasized the existence of a structural problem requiring a holistic and not a one-time response. As a result, the government outlined a strategy to clean up the sector by encouraging mergers and takeovers. The logic was this: by joining with larger entities, available resources would be increased and the possible capital needs of weaker institutions would be covered. All this would also minimize the use of public funds. The process of mergers and acquisitions from 2009 altered the Spanish banking landscape, especially in terms of savings banks, most of which were transformed into banks.

The established format for that process worked through the Institutional Protection System, also known as 'cold merger'. In essence, its design consisted of forming with the savings banks a holding company with a new leading entity, but maintaining their respective boards of directors and corporate images.

Far from avoiding recourse to public funds, that process ultimately meant a drain on money set aside for bailing out financial institutions. Among other issues, the process itself was more concerned with safeguarding controlling interests over entities than with determining the magnitude of the problem and seeking a solution. In addition, the merger process was done without considering the most basic due-diligence analysis of such transactions, the clearest example being the case of Caja Madrid with Bancaja (along with other smaller entities) into Banco Financiero y de Ahorros (BFA), the holding company of Bankia. In essence, this was a matter of joining two of the institutions that were most exposed to toxic real estate assets into a larger company. The result was nothing less than the largest nationalization of a private entity in Spain's history, and the action ended in court due to various irregularities ranging from Bankia's stock market flotation to the falsification of the accounts that led to its bailout.

The dilapidation of public resources used in these measures kept intact the capital of bondholders and other creditors so that they assumed no burden in the recapitalization. The idea was, again, to preserve confidence and to avoid a bank run, but matters of substance were again eluded (although now they had been identified: the accumulation of damaged assets on bank balance sheets and the solvency risk, not just liquidity risk.

The bailout of BFA-Bankia in 2012 marked the turning point in the sector's restructuring policies. The capital that this entity required and Spain's risk premium were both so high that the new government was forced to request a credit line of up to €100 billion from the EU.[14] The counterpart was the signing of a memorandum of understanding which, among other conditions, required the creation of a 'bad bank' with a majority of private capital (whose mission was to acquire from banks those assets and loan portfolios considered most problematic). The memorandum of understanding also required an external audit of the banking system and the elaboration of stress tests by an entity outside the BoS.

The ECB also treated the banking crisis as a liquidity problem, in part because it lacked supervisory powers (which it would not assume until November 2014). In addition, the ECB did not want to affect bank bondholders for fear of aggravating the recession, which paradoxically contributed to consolidating it.

Thus, in the face of the collapse of the interbank market, the ECB began long-term financing operations (LTRO). That move eliminated limits on liquidity auctions to banks ('full allotment') and extended the redemption period from 3 to 36 months, gradually lowering the ECB's financing costs from an initial 2% in 2009 to 0% in March 2016.

This mechanism was a lifeline for the European banking system in general, and the Spanish system in particular: the sector flocked to the auctions. In the case of Spain, this process helped to reduce its risk premium due to the greater demand for Spanish public bonds, which served as collateral for accessing ECB financing. But this decline in the risk premium was due to purchases of public debt by local banks, not to rising international confidence. The problem with the mechanism was that by significantly increasing the holdings of government securities in the banks' balance sheets, systemic risk increased via the tightening of links between the banking crisis and the sovereign crisis. This factor encouraged the bullish spiral of Spain's risk premium to its zenith in the summer of 2012.

The ECB's commitment to intervene by all available means to preserve the euro served to ease tension and to improve access to international liquidity. Furthermore, the financial bailout in Spain allowed the recapitalization of banking institutions in a perilous situation, especially the aforementioned BFA-Bankia. But as this case clearly demonstrates, the facilitation of liquidity does not heal solvency problems. It only buys time.

Other factors that have worked in favor of improved banking soundness include the Spanish economy's growth since 2014, which has contributed to the timely reactivation of new credit, especially for the purchase of durable consumer goods (although credit stock has continued to decline). However, this recovery has helped to reduce household leverage, which has made greater efforts to reduce levels of indebtedness (although the percentage of dubious loans remains above 2012 levels).

Nevertheless, the Spanish banking sector remains in a very delicate state due to three fundamental factors. First, the private debt of families and companies, although significantly lower than before, continues to be high. According to calculations from BoS data, debt was at 66.7% of GDP for households and at 102.3% for non-financial corporations in June 2016. Second, the balance sheet recession resulting from overindebtedness has generated a 'liquidity trap' in which rates have remained low to avoid recession, but without serving to boost credit. The policy of massive purchases of securities by the ECB has made it cheaper to finance banks, companies, and households alike, but has not improved the solvency of demand in the context of an unemployment rate still above 18% in 2017 (INE), poor job quality, and a decline in the purchasing power of the population at large. Finally, the lack of solvent credit and the narrow margins that allow interest rates to remain at historical lows have complicated the profitability of the banks, which have reacted by carrying out staff restructurings and office closures.

Socialization of losses

The bailout made by the state through 2016 amounted to €53,553 million: 5.2% of GDP.[15] To date, only 5% of that public aid has been recovered: €2,686 million. To this aid in form of capital must be added the guarantees granted by the state to credit institutions, as well as public guarantees in the purchase of entities, through APS. These guarantees amount to €110,895 million, of which 99% (€109,836 million) had already been cancelled by 2016.

In cases of divestment from entities by the public sector, we must also consider the additional guarantees granted to the financial entities that acquired them. Of the total amount disbursed, a further €963 million should be added to the FROB, as well as extraordinary loans for certain restructuring processes, granted by the BoS (€9.8 billion) or by the FROB itself (€6.5 billion). All balances have been cancelled. Lastly, we must add the public funds contributed as capital to the 'bad bank', known as the Asset Management Company for Bank Restructuring (SAREB by its Spanish acronym).

As a result, public aid in the form of capital, with an impact on the budget deficit, has cost 5.2% of the GDP of 2015. This is without consideration of the socialization of risk that these various forms of public guarantee represent. According to Eurostat data, in 2014, Spain was the country with the third-highest volume of guarantees in force; granted to the financial sector as a percentage of GDP (12.5%), Spain's guarantees were surpassed only by Ireland and Greece (at 13.3% and 24.3% of GDP, respectively).

Until 2014, only five Eurozone countries recorded a higher crisis-related cost than the Spanish bailout: Ireland (26.7% of GDP), Greece (12.7%), Slovenia (10.9%), Cyprus (10.6%), and Portugal (6.8%), compared to 4.9% for Spain (Maurer and Grussenmayer, 2015), which shows that the Spanish banking system was not as sound as it appeared at the beginning of the crisis.

The case of SAREB, mentioned earlier, is noteworthy, as this company was created in order to remove problematic real estate assets from the banks' balance sheets, which in the end meant treating the banking crisis as a solvency problem. With the purchase of 'toxic' assets, a conflict arose between two options. The lower the purchase, the greater the loss that the banks would have to recognize, which could lead to further recapitalizations. Too high a price would make it more difficult for SAREB to recover the investment. This entity, following the model of the Irish 'bad bank' (NAMA) designed by the ECB, has a majority of private capital (55%), with the remaining 45% publicly owned by the FROB. In order to attract investors, it was necessary to offer expectations of profitability at the cost of the socialization of losses, to be assumed by the state. In this respect, average potential returns were offered at between 14% and 15%.

In any case, a positive net effect would be possible to the extent that toxic assets were effectively removed from the balance sheets of the banks, which would lead to a recovery of confidence and facilitate the granting of new credit. However, the main investors in SAREB are in fact other local banks: Santander (16.6%), CaixaBank (12.2%), Banc Sabadell (6.61%), Banco Popular (5.6%), and Kutxabank (2.5%), among others.[16] Thus, although (logically) none of the banks with acquired assets is a shareholder of SAREB, the toxic assets remain in the banking sector, which calls the whole process into question.

The accounting soundness of SAREB depends on the state of the real estate market, which remains far from recovering its pre-crisis levels. As a result, SAREB has been recording large losses since its inception. According to its annual report for 2016, pre-tax losses for the year totaled €663 million (with negative balances of €472 million in 2015, €804 million in 2014, €1,603 million in 2013, and €5.5 million in 2012). Therefore, accumulated losses amounted to about €3,186 million in just five years. Because its bond issue is guaranteed by the state and, as noted, the institution has not been detached from the financial system, we are facing a potential time bomb for public-sector finance.

All these different mechanisms deployed in order to help or support the financial system therefore shifted the risk and/or cost from the private banking sector to the public sector. Not only was the private debt crisis socialized, but its costs were distributed regressively among the population, because the measures applied to prioritize reduction of the budget deficit and the public debt were based mainly on strategies to slightly increase progressive taxes and on the reduction of social spending (as will be seen in Chapter 5). In addition, the main bank creditors were protected, as no efforts were made to ascertain responsibilities for the increase in the Spanish public debt.

All this has contributed to reducing private-sector debt in parallel with the debt increase in the public sector. However, as mentioned, the huge increase in Spanish public debt was mainly due to the fall in public revenues and, to a lesser extent, the increase in public spending due to automatic stabilizers, which led to the appearance of budgetary deficits. At the same time, the stock of private debt began to decline (albeit very slowly) due to the need for deleveraging of companies and households, a typical feature in a balance sheet recession. As a result, between December 2007 and 2015, non-financial private debt went from 245.7% to 173.1% of GDP and public debt increased over the same period, from 35.5% in 2007 to 99.98% of GDP at the end of 2016 (BoE).

In the end, the bailout shifted the risk that existed in the financial sector to the public sector through an increase in the cost of public debt. At the same time, a large part of the bonds issued by the state has been bought by the same national private banks that were aided by the public sector, especially during the risk premium crisis (between 2010 and 2012[17]), thus perpetuating the vicious circle referred to earlier.

Conclusions

This chapter allows us to draw some conclusions, as much on the crisis itself as on the conditions and prospects for the Spanish economy. To begin with, it is important to highlight the relevance of factors, identified as vulnerabilities, typical of the Spanish economy. Although the debt crisis was a worldwide event, Spain's peculiarity can contribute critical characteristics to our understanding of the severity of the crisis. In addition, the vulnerability factors here detected were not limited to the financial sphere, but ranged to other areas, including the country's fragile external insertion or the weak productive structure of its economy, as referred to in the first two chapters. Taking this into consideration, the hypothetical task of engaging in a process of economic transformation that can overcome these weaknesses and substantially reduce the vulnerability of the Spanish economy will require action in areas beyond finance.

Another line of reflection concerns the role of the EMU in shaping Spanish financial vulnerability. Although this analysis has not focused on that question, it does support the fact that EMU membership has proved to be an aggravating factor, both in the excessive use of (external) debt during the expansionary period and in the constraints on implementation of an appropriate crisis management strategy.

Finally, Spain's strategy of crisis management, strongly conditioned by the economic and institutional restrictions imposed by EMU membership, bears reviewing. In this respect, three lessons can be drawn from our analysis. In the first place, the strategy followed was based on a misdiagnosis of the situation, focused on liquidity problems in the financial sector and without addressing issues of solvency, which affect not only the financial sector but also a good part of the non-financial sector.

Second, and largely derived from the initial misdiagnosis, management of the crisis has been ineffective, both in terms of quickly resolving the private debt crisis and of laying foundations so that such a dynamic of overindebtedness will not happen again. Beyond inefficiency, taking into account the perverse effects of fiscal austerity programs on the desired reactivation of demand, the desired capacity to generate employment and income, and the possibility of rapidly effecting a deleveraging process, we can say that management of the debt crisis has been counterproductive.

Third, in addition to being ineffective and counterproductive, we should end up by emphasizing the marked regressive nature of this strategy. The socialization of private losses, and also a socialization of risk though public guarantees on private liabilities, along with the subsequent application of austerity programs (as will be discussed in Chapter 5) has specially affected those social groups that had nothing to do with the causes of the crisis, and that were the least prepared, in terms of resources, to face it.

Notes

1 Author names are given in alphabetical order, as all share equal responsibility for this chapter.
2 In Spain, there are three types of deposit institutions: banks, savings banks, and credit unions. The legal reforms approved after the crisis, especially Decree Law 6/2010 of April 9, prompted many savings banks to merge and transform into banks until they were reduced to a minimal presence.

3 Savings banks could not be acquired partially or totally due to the absence of defined legal property (although they were subject to private law). In addition, they could not issue shares or increase capital.

4 The holding company Argentaria was created in 1991 and was partially privatized in 1993 by the Felipe González administration (PSOE); later, under the José Maria Aznar administration (PP), it was sold to Banco Bilbao Vizcaya, creating Banco Bilbao Vizcaya Argentaria (BBVA).

5 Spanish financial integration materialized with its membership into the European Monetary System (EMS) in 1989, 10 years after that system's creation.

6 Law 13/1994 of June 1. It should be pointed out that it lacked full autonomy in some respects, including banking supervision, which was subject to the Ministry of Economy. At present, such oversight is performed by the European Central Bank (ECB).

7 According to data from the European Mortgage Federation (EMF), the average price of housing increased by a cumulative 115.2% during 1996–2007. Inflation of real estate assets was not exclusive to Spain, nor to the Eurozone. The increase of residential housing prices from 1997 to 2005 reached 73% in the United States, 114% in Australia, 154% in the UK, 192% in Ireland, and 244% in South Africa (*The Economist*, June 16, 2005).

8 This made possible the avoidance of regulatory rules on loan to value, which sets a ceiling on the mortgage loan at 80% of the appraisal value of the property (Jiménez-Ridruejo Ayuso, 2014: 161).

9 Authors' calculations from BoS and National Accounts (SNI).

10 Even in 2012, when the public expenditure reached its highest value, Spain's public spending was at 47.2% of GDP, compared with 49.9% in the overall Eurozone and 49.3% in the EU (Source: Eurostat).

11 This was 3.1% and 2.8% of GDP in 2015 and 2016, respectively. Although this financial burden was less than 5% in 1995, it had increased from 1.6% in 2008 (Eurostat data).

12 Such was the 'E Plan' (the Spanish Plan for the Stimulation of Economy and Employment), which consisted of a set of measures aimed mainly (but not only) at public works managed by municipalities in order to counteract strong job losses in the construction sector. The cost of this plan was modest: €12,836 million (or 1.2% of 2009 GDP), distributed in two parts (€7,836 million in 2008 and €5,000 million more in 2009).

13 The justification was registered in the reformed constitutional text itself. Article 135, paragraph 2, reads as follows: 'The present economic and financial situation has only strengthened the principle of reference to our Constitution.' The official position of the government at the time was that 'there was no other option' (*El País*, August 30, 2011).

14 In July 2012, the interest rate on the 10-year Spanish bond was approaching 7%. At that time, with massive capital flights and the soundness of the Spanish banking system challenged, the recourse to markets for the state to finance the recapitalization of Bankia proved enormously expensive. For this reason, the conservative government of President Mariano Rajoy chose to request a financial bailout from Brussels.

15 This refers to public aid computable as capital made through the FROB. The total aid between 2009 and 2016 amounts to €61,495 million, of which €7,942 million has been contributed by the banking industry through the Deposit Guarantee Fund. The state plans to spend another €1.1 billion in 2017, the net amount of the bailout being €48,228 million (at the time of writing), according to BoS data.

16 Among the partners are Deutsche Bank, several national and foreign insurance companies, and the real estate branch of the energy company Iberdrola (First Semester Activity Report, 2016, of the SAREB).

17 Financial institutions reduced their exposure to Spanish public debt until the change in ECB monetary policy in 2012. Thus, in August 2016, 50.8% of state debt was held by non-resident creditors (Bulletin of Statistics of the Spanish Public Treasury, September 2016).

References

Analistas Financieros Internacionales (AFI) (2012): *Guía del Sistema Financiero Español*. Madrid: Ediciones Empresa Global.

Delgado, J., Saurina, J. and Towsend, R. (2008): 'Estrategias de expansión de las entidades de depósito españolas: Una primera aproximación descriptiva', *Estabilidad Financiera*, 15, pp. 99–118.

European Mortgage Federation (EMF) (2016): *Hypostat. A Review of Mortgage and Housing Markets*, Brussels: EMF.

Fisher, I. (1933): 'The Debt-Deflation Theory of Great Depression', *Econometrica*, 1 (4), pp. 337–357.

Jiménez-Ridruejo Ayuso, Z. (2014): 'El comportamiento del sector financiero, su crisis y sus repercusiones', in N.E. García and S.M. Ruesga (coords.), *¿Qué ha pasado en la economía española? La Gran Recesión 2.0 (2008–2013)*, Madrid: Anaya, pp. 151–185.

Kalecki, M. (1971): *Selected Essays on the Dynamics of the Capitalist Economy (1933–1970)*, London: Cambridge University Press.

Keen, S. (2011): *Debunking Economics. The Naked Emperor Dethroned*, Revised and Expanded Edition. London: Zed Books.

Keynes, J.M. (1936): *A General Theory of Employment, Interest and Money*, New York: Prometheus Books, 2002.

Koo, R. (2011): 'The World in Balance Sheet Recession: Causes, Cure and Politics', *Real World Economics Review*, 58, pp. 19–37.

Lago Peñas, M. (2012): 'El gasto público: un falso culpable', *Informes de la Fundación Primero de Mayo*, 46, Madrid: Fundación Primero de Mayo.

Maurer, H. and Grussenmeyer, P. (2015): 'Financial Assistance Measures in the Euro Area from 2008 to 2013: Statistical Framework and Fiscal Impact', *Statistics Paper Series (European Central Bank)*, 7.

Medialdea, B. and A. Sanabria (2013): 'La financiarización de la economía mundial: hacia una caracterización', *Revista de Economía Mundial*, 32, pp. 195–227.

Minsky, H. (1992): 'The Financial Instability Hypothesis', *Working Paper (Levy Economics Institute)*, 74.

Moore, B.J. (1988): 'The Endogenous Money Supply', *Journal of Post Keynesian Economics*, 10 (3), pp. 372–385.

Palazuelos, E. and Fernández, R. (2007): 'La tasa de beneficio en la dinámica económica de los países europeos, 1984–2003', *Estudios de Economía Aplicada*, 25 (3), pp. 901–926.

Sanabria, A. (2012): 'La crisis del euro y la dictadura de los acreedores', *Momento Económico*, 23–24., pp. 17–28.

Sanabria, A. and Medialdea, B. (2016): 'Lending Calling. Recession by Over-Indebtedness: Description add Specific Features of the Spanish Case', *Panoeconomicus*, 63 (2), pp. 195–210.

Vilariño, Á. (2001): *Sistema financiero español*. Madrid: Akal.

Wray, L.R. (1990): *Money and Credit in Capitalist Economies: The Endogenous Money Approach*, Aldershoty Brookfield: Edward Elgar.

4 The Spanish labor market

On the path of flexibility and wage devaluation

*María Eugenia Ruiz-Gálvez
and Lucía Vicent Valverde*[1]

Introduction

In the preceding chapters, we have shown the fundamentals of the process of growth, crisis, and adjustment in its three main dimensions: the accumulation pattern, external insertion, and financial capital. With this chapter, the objective of which is to study the labor market, we begin a second analytical segment that focuses on the effects of prior dynamics on the structure of labor relations, both before and during the recession. Once this question has been considered, Chapter 5 will deal with the outcome of the distributive struggle, thus completing our portrait of what has happened in the Spanish economy.

The Spanish labor market has been characterized in recent decades by enormous and growing imbalances. Although the current crisis has highlighted increased levels of unemployment and high rates of temporality, among other aspects that underline the growing precariousness of jobs, the fact remains that during the previous stage, worrisome particularities of the Spanish labor market had already made it different from other European nations. Through the last third of the twentieth century, Spain had been exhibiting major structural problems in the field of employment, to which new challenges have now been added (segmentation among workers, wage devaluation, degradation of contractual forms, etc.). All these factors increasingly exacerbate tensions and compromise the options for guaranteeing good working conditions.

Here we address the central aspects that have altered Spain's labor market, surveying the transformations that have occurred in the framework of labor relations and their main consequences. In the first section, we describe the analytical elements of the economic context that have most influenced the labor market during recent decades, applying an aggregate perspective that allows us to place Spain within the European Union (EU). Issues such as membership in the EU or the peculiarities of Spain's historical legacy are significant factors that have shaped the current labor framework, and we touch on these matters while studying the main labor policies and business strategies around employment. In the second section, we analyze the more recent period marked by recession and the application of policies directly affecting the labor relations model, recognizing elements of both departure from and continuity with prior periods. To conclude, we reflect on the main consequences of the adjustment policies deployed in the years of the current economic crisis.

Model and structure of labor relations in Spain

From our analytical perspective, it is assumed that within the capitalist economic system, the labor market has undergone significant changes in response to certain demands for increased private profits and capital accumulation, as discussed in Chapter 1. The adoption of entrepreneurial strategies not always contemporaneous or consistent with those of other national scenarios, along with a regulatory framework that has allowed for their application, has transferred labor relations to the global scale, and traditional characteristics of employment have been adjusted to better meet the imperative of profitability (De Serres et al., 2001; Gaffard and Sarraceno, 2009).

From the end of the Second World War to the 1970s, the European employment standard showed a pattern of stability, low levels of unemployment, and a positive evolution of wages, aspects capable of guaranteeing a peaceful social climate by meeting certain demands of the labor movement without compromising the demands of capital accumulation. At the onset of the crisis of the 1970s, economic growth began to fall and unemployment rates in Europe rose, jeopardizing both the model of employment and the principles of productive organization seen in the previous period (Piore and Sabel, 1990).

In this emerging scenario, new business strategies were articulated and technological advances were applied that modified existing forms of labor organization and traditional norms of employment, and external competitiveness became the prime condition for the survival of companies. One facet of competitiveness focused on flexible response to any 'rigidities' detected in a given labor market.[2] Apart from rare exceptions that combined this new dogma of flexibility with social coverage,[3] the applied measures tended to move in one direction: toward the dismantling or reduction of labor rights conquered in previous decades (Streeck, 1988; Fina, 2001; González and Guillén, 2009).[4]

In the case of Spain, one finds clear distinctions from processes followed by neighboring countries. The conditions that determined the aftermath of the Francoist regime postponed the effects of the 1970s crisis and created a labor market with its own peculiar traits (Miguélez, 1995; Sola, 2014). Elements inherited from that time still explain, to a considerable extent, the current structure of labor relations. Despite the definition of Spain's pre-democratic model as rigid, in truth certain elements provided flexibility in labor relations: a minimum wage so low that it could scarcely affect wage relationships, special premiums used as a method of rewarding employees in selective and discriminatory ways, abuse of overtime, and meager unemployment benefits. This was a regime that suppressed any 'distorting'[5] variable (including the prohibition of trade unions), with the aim of reducing and subordinating social power and establishing a low-wage economy (Sola, 2010).

With the death of Franco in 1975, a complex and delicate stage of transition began in which persistent aspects of the previous era were combined with post-Francoist transformations. This was a period marked both by factors intrinsic to a political change of this magnitude and by external factors (such as the international oil crisis or the entry into the European Economic Community [EEC]), with major consequences for Spain's labor market and labor relations. The new democratic parliamentary parties agreed on pillars of economic and employment policy with the signing of the Moncloa Pacts in 1977. This agreement served as the epicenter of the development of the welfare state, the democratization of social relations, the legalization of trade unions, and the construction of a framework for labor rights. But it also constituted a plan of adjustment to guarantee business profitability and to combat imbalances that prevented the country from meeting certain requirements for inclusion in the EEC.

In this scenario, a new political and social framework was created, but elements of the Franco legacy were maintained. The fact that the new approach failed to promote a process of industrial restructuring, opting instead for a process of de-industrialization, promoted a growth model based on sectors offering little added value (tourism and construction) and of low technological degree that continue to cause Spain to lag behind other European players (Fina and Toharia, 1987; López and Malo, 2015). In this way, a model of labor relations was consolidated that was flexible and adaptable to the EU framework requirements, but which acquired its own characteristics in the Spanish economy (Miguélez and Prieto, 2009).

Given this, and our objective of understanding the structure and dynamics of labor relations in Spain, we shall analyze three fundamental aspects: i) the structure of the industrial relations model and changes to business strategies and labor policies; (ii) the role of trade unions and other actors involved in employment; and (iii) the effects on the labor market.

The structure of the model of labor relations in Spain: labor policies and business strategies

The development of low-productivity sectors (as discussed in Chapters 1 and 2) consolidated a low-wage labor market and precarious working conditions, but these elements have been functional to the ideological discourse of flexibility, as well as to the dismantling of the labor movement and the de-legitimation of the union struggle. As we can see, the distance that separates Spain in occupational distribution by sector with respect to the EU is significant and, comparatively speaking, helps us to understand certain particularities of Spain's labor market and to explain (at least in part) ongoing structural problems (Table 4.1).

The weight of jobs in strategic sectors with greater technological and productivity potential (as in some manufacturing industries), or in sectors that demand higher qualification and specialization (as with qualified services), present in Spain a clear deficit with respect to the European aggregate. On the other hand, overrepresented activities include those with atypical contracting modalities (temporary and part-time and with degraded labor conditions) which have acquired greater relative weight, along with other more precarious forms of paid work. Thus, the agrarian and construction sectors (presented in aggregate because they combine

Table 4.1 Distribution of occupations in the EU-15 and Spain, 1995, 2007, and 2015 (%)

	UE15			Spain		
	1995	2007	2015	1995	2007	2015
Agriculture and construction	12.70	11.40	9.10	18.30	17.60	10.10
Agriculture and fishery	4.80	3.20	2.50	8.70	4.40	4.10
Construction	7.90	8.20	6.60	9.70	13.20	6.00
Manufacturing industry	21.30	17.10	14.30	19.40	15.20	12.50
Qualified services and non-manufacturing industry	41.40	45.80	50.40	32.70	33.00	44.70
Extractive industry	0.40	0.30	0.20	0.50	0.30	0.20
Energy and utilities	0.90	0.70	0.60	0.80	0.60	1.30
Transport, storage, and logistics	6.10	6.00	8.10	6.10	5.80	7.90
Financial intermediation	3.50	3.30	3.20	2.60	2.50	2.50
Public administration, defense, and social security	7.90	7.40	7.00	6.50	6.10	7.40
Real estate and business rental services	6.90	10.60	11.30	5.40	6.10	10.70
Education	6.60	7.00	7.80	5.70	5.50	6.60
Health activities and social services	9.10	10.60	12.20	5.10	6.10	8.10
Other services	24.20	25.20	24.70	29.50	30.30	30.60
Trade and repair services	15.00	14.40	14.00	16.50	15.30	16.30
Hostelry	3.80	4.60	5.10	6.50	7.10	8.40
Other activities and personal social services	4.50	4.90	4.40	3.80	4.20	2.40
Domestic service	0.90	1.30	1.20	2.80	3.70	3.50

Note: Data for 1995 and 2007 from NACE Rev. 1.1; data for 2015 from NACE Rev. 2.

Source: Own elaboration with data from Eurostat (Labor Force Survey).

certain labor characteristics, including low security, seasonality, low qualification, lower remuneration, and flexible distribution of days) are weighted well above EU levels.

Services present a similar situation. By distinguishing those that require lower levels of training and qualification (and that fall into the category of 'other services') from those where occupation profiles are more specific (where professional trajectories are safer and higher salaries are guaranteed, offering better conditions in general), the data for Spain show a higher job concentration in the former category.

The dynamics followed by occupational specialization in Spain are defined by features that have deepened the problems of the past. Job creation during the last expansionary period (1995–2007) concentrated mainly on construction and services, especially in the financial bubble sector. When the crisis erupted, these sectorial branches were affected by sharp job destruction, especially among the less skilled. The behavior of employment in Spain has been marked by a strong pro-cyclical character; despite job creation during times of economic growth, the tendency in recessive stages has been to expel increasing numbers from the labor market. This process has been concentrated in sectors where the temporality rates exceed the European average, where wages are also below the average, and where schedule flexibility and intensity of work are greater than in other activities,[6] and this in turn increases inequalities among workers and makes employees more vulnerable to job loss.

It should be noted that it is precisely in such occupational niches that Spain is above the EU-15 average, where trade union presence and bargaining power are lower and where the mobilization of trade unions is more complex. Because these are employment spaces where long periods of precariousness are combined with unemployment, multi-employment has become increasingly standardized as a strategy to achieve sufficient wage income, and unfavorable temporary, part-time, or socially scheduled hiring is quite common. In short, these are spaces where jobs are of lower quality, marked by class identity and strong fragmentation (Pitxer and Sánchez, 2008).

Concurrent with this evolution in occupational specialization, the regulatory framework was adapted to the needs of the productive model, progressively moving the market risks towards employment and thus facilitating the expulsion of workers from jobs and increasing the sensitivity of jobs to business cycles. In the case of the Spanish economy, we have observed an intensive process of legislative change that suits the relaxation of labor relations. Since the adoption of the Workers' Statute (Estatuto de los Trabajadores in Spanish, or ET) in 1980, 11 reforms and more than 40 labor decrees have been passed. As can be seen in Figure 4.1, these have occurred over recent decades regardless of the existing government – whether Unión de Centro Democrático (UCD), Partido Socialista Obrero Español (PSOE), or Partido Popular (PP).

These various strategies have a shared common goal: labor deregulation.[7] The process has been structural in nature, and the applied reforms[8] that have sought to make wage relations more flexible (as a mechanism to overcome 'obstacles' that prevent a balance between job supply and demand) have materialized in two areas, through social partnership and in companies.

First, social partnership (with collective bargaining taking place at the local, intermediate, and state levels) develops policies on conditions of employment and other aspects related to deferred salaries and collective bargaining. Most policies included within such legislative reforms have focused on intensifying external flexibility, creating tools to speed entry into the labor market and to reduce the costs of exit, meanwhile reducing social benefits, pensions, and/or subsidies.[9] The main objective has been to create the necessary mechanisms to adapt the workforce, by increasing or decreasing employment, to changes in the economic situation without incurring high costs. The results have been questionable, judging by the evolution of unemployment rates that have struggled without reaching the EU-15 average and have never dropped below 8%.

Since the first Labor Reform, in 1984, adopted measures have focused on easing contractual modalities and reducing dismissal costs, with the ultimate aim of improving employment levels, regardless of their quality. One path towards labor deregulation eased a prior ban on temporality, eliminating the principle of causality and any restrictions that could represent an obstacle to the needs of capital.

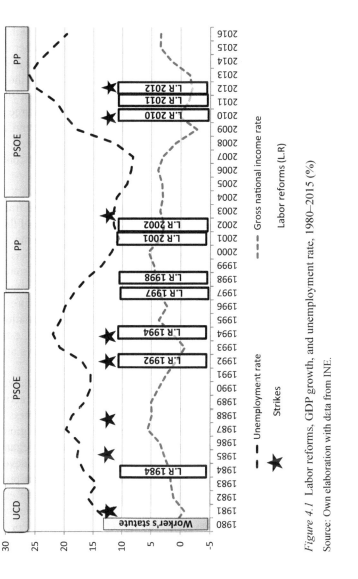

Figure 4.1 Labor reforms, GDP growth, and unemployment rate, 1980–2015 (%)

Source: Own elaboration with data from INE.

New flexible contractual forms were also promoted, including contracts for a specific job or service, training contracts, part-time contracts, and subcontracting.

Consequently, high rates of temporality have played a role in the job dynamic. According to data provided by Eurostat, the percentage of temporary workers has been extraordinarily high in the Spanish economy: over the past three decades, about 30% to 35% of wage earners had a temporary contractual relationship (20 percentage points above the EU-15 average). The evolution and promotion of temporality as a recruitment strategy have become other structural problems in the labor relations framework. Alongside temporality, part-time work has gained importance in recent decades as a consequence of the growing service sector and adaptability to demands for current forms of organizing work, especially for women and young people. While in the 1980s part-time employment remained under 5% (compared to an EU-wide average of around 10%), by the end of the 1990s it had doubled, and that increase has not abated (as it has in most EU economies). Far from slowing, this type of recruitment continues to increase steadily.

Within this area of contract, the current labor relations framework provides that collective agreements, negotiated by the most representative trade union organizations, may affect all workers in the same field, irrespective of their affiliation (or not) with these organizations. During the 1990s, the coverage rate was around 79% to 80%. In the period just before the outbreak of the crisis, in 2007, approximately 85% to 82% of salaried workers were protected by some collective agreement. However, since the Labor Reform of 2012, the coverage rate has declined, whereas new, precarious contractual forms have gained. At present, only 75% of workers are protected by some agreement, whereas negotiation procedures and the importance of collective bargaining to labor and wage terms are not widely understood among the working class and are not always applied by business organizations.

At the same time, internal and wage flexibility measures have allowed workforce and labor costs to be adapted to the needs of whatever specific activity they engage in. Throughout recent decades, processes of change in business and production have been marked by outsourcing and fragmentation (Mingione, 1993; Castillo, 2005). In the 1980s and 1990s, the Spanish economy began a complex process of de-industrialization that was accompanied by the development and implementation of new organizational methods known as lean production, outsourcing, or just-in-time production.[10] These strategies have been essentially based on the fragmentation of tasks and activities previously integrated into a single chain or production process, with the objective of favoring profitability and competitiveness through permanent cost reduction and the intensification of work (Boyer and Freyssenet, 2003). To this end, the adaptability of labor to different tasks, the de-specialization of work, the possibility of increasing or reducing the working schedule (blocks of days, overtime, rotating shifts . . .), temporary suspensions of activities, and wage moderation have been among the recurrent mechanisms found in business strategies, aimed at maintaining or increasing profit margins – all thanks to the application of legislative reforms.

These new methods of organizing work and production have not only transformed business structures and inter-firm dynamics; they have also shaped the social relations of employment by segmenting the working class and by modifying political and trade union actions in the workplace. The polarization in working conditions and the transformation of working-class identities are two direct effects of fragmentation and the new division of labor that have posed a continuing challenge to trade union organizations (Blanco, 2004; Baylos, 2014).

The role of trade unions and collective bargaining

Indeed, changes in the productive structure and transformations in the world of employment are both characteristic of recent decades, particularly in the case of the Spanish economy. Such changes to the rules of the game have conditioned the strategies and the role of trade unions and have served as an indicator of the changing relations between private capital and wage labor. From the sphere of social partnership, where the different social agents (unions, companies, government) interact, trade union activity has been highly conditioned and limited by economic, political, and social events.

Although the 1980s were years of confrontation and stagnation in terms of social dialogue (see Figure 4.1), the crisis of the 1990s had a moderating effect, and until the Interconfederal Agreement for Collective Bargaining in 2002 and the Declaration for Social Dialogue in 2004, no relevant milestones emerged in this area. Both agreements included the need to improve the quality of employment, to promote vocational training and qualification, to introduce gender equality criteria, and to increase occupational safety and health mechanisms, among other measures. Both reflected the need to prioritize social dialogue and to broaden the scope of collective bargaining, which served as an ethical code, but their real effects were very limited (Pitxer and Sánchez, 2008).[11] Despite the adverse scenario under which the unions operate, weak results give proof that efforts made by unions have not been sufficient to achieve the objectives set out in these agreements.

Similarly, in the ambit of businesses and workplaces, where union organizations are closer to workers, strategies have not shown satisfactory evolution. Data from the European Observatory for Industrial Relations and the Ministry of Employment and Social Security (MESS) show that Spain's union membership has always been among the lowest in Europe. Although it had increased from the 1980s until the mid-1990s, it suffered a certain decline during the expansionary period and again following the outbreak of the current crisis, keeping Spain at the tail end of European affiliation rankings (Table 4.2).[12]

Going deeper into these data, there are several areas where union strategies fail to show strength. The groups with lower union representation coincide with those already subject to the most precarious working conditions (women, youth, and immigrant populations).[13]

Likewise, if we analyze the rate of union affiliation at the sectorial and business levels, the data available for the years 2006–2010 show several elements

Table 4.2 Union membership rate, 1980–2014 (% of total wage earners)

	1980	1985	1990	1995	2000	2005	2010	2014
Union membership rate	13.5	12.6	13.5	16.8	16.6	14.6	17.3	16.1

Source: European Observatory for Industrial Relations and Ministry of Employment and Social Security (MESS).

of continuity. On the one hand, in work centers with fewer workers, the difficulty or even the legal impossibility of obtaining union representation are greater; therefore, there are many companies where collective action never arrives. On the other hand, trade unions such as in industry, transport, or manufacturing, as well as those under public ownership, especially health services, education, and public administration, have traditionally had greater membership than other branches and activities. Contrarily, the sectors with the highest incidence of precarious work (such as hospitality, tourism, or those related to care) are those in which union membership is much lower.[14] It should be added that the working class in general has little knowledge of union activity within a given company. According to the average of surveys carried out by the Ministry of Labor, more than 30% know nothing about how unions operate, and only 13% know something of the work done by trade union organizations.

As has been pointed out, trade union action has been greatly affected by several factors. The diversity of identities within the working class and the process of de-industrialization, together with fragmentation, subcontracting, and labor segmentation, all contribute to the reduced role and weakening of unions, as does the transformation of historical bases on which unions were sustained. The most vulnerable groups of workers and the most precarious working spaces are far removed from union activity and collective struggle. Given this reality, it comes as no surprise that the balance of forces between capital and labor has been tremendously affected in favor of the former.

Consequences of the model

Beyond the issues mentioned, such as those relating to unemployment or temporary employment rates, it is important to analyze certain effects of the industrial relations model, and in particular the effects on wages. Wage evolution, contrary to those who would insist on holding wages accountable for the loss of competitiveness (as seen in Chapter 2), has tended towards stagnation and with decreasing rates of change from decade to decade (Figure 4.2).

Whereas in other EU countries real wages began to manifest lower rates of variation from the 1970s, in the case of Spain this process did not become clear until the beginning of the 1980s. Since then, and except for periods of greater labor conflict, the decline has at times reached negative levels below the period of the pre-crisis growth stage; following an initial period characterized by the expulsion

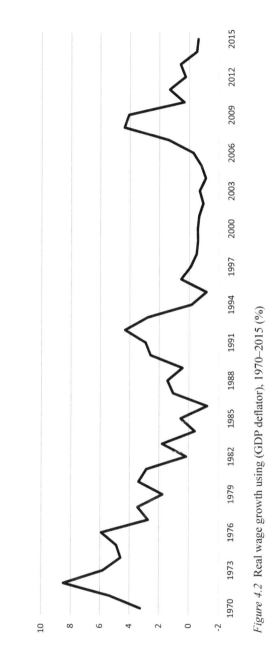

Figure 4.2 Real wage growth using (GDP deflator), 1970–2015 (%)

Source: Own elaboration with data from AMECO.

of workers with the lowest wages, stagnation returned and the rates of variation again show negative values. Resulting from this evolution has been a decrease in the weight of wages in terms of GDP, as we will see in Chapter 5.

In addition to the effect on wages, another impact has been the intensification of work. Clearly, the work-time factor is a key variable for the flexible management of companies. Based on information from the Labor Conditions Surveys carried out from the mid-1990s to 2011, there has been an increasing tendency to prolong the working day (with or without additional economic compensation), as well as an increase in work rates in terms of speed, greater rigidity of task execution, reduction of construction and delivery periods, and a higher instance of multi-tasking, in over 44% of respondents. Some authors define this process as in line with a 'tense flow' or stress management model (Durand, 2011; Castillo and López Calle, 2009), referring to the consequences of incorporating methods that adjust to demand at the expense of workers and the character of their jobs.

Crisis and adjustment in the Spanish labor market

From the outbreak of the crisis in 2008, the labor panorama in Spain may be characterized as an intensification of adjustments that have been taking place for several decades and whose main features have been highlighted in the previous section.

Main effects of the crisis

One of the most important direct effects has been the strong destruction of employment. As we have seen, Spain was already subject to structural problems in terms of unemployment. Although during the expansionary period unemployment dropped significantly, in comparison with the 1990s, the weak underlying structure of the labor market has since been exposed to the exponential growth of unemployment at rates well above the EU average. This unemployment has been especially alarming for younger populations, which exceeded 50% of the overall unemployed population in 2012 and 2013 (Figure 4.3), as well as that of immigrant populations, as verified by the National Institute of Statistics (in Spanish, INE).

If we analyze this trend, we see that construction and industry have been the branches of activity most affected by unemployment (branches with a higher proportion of male workers, where large portions of the immigrant population have worked since the beginning of the century and where workers have low levels of training). Those most vulnerable to changes in the early days of the recession (young people and immigrants) have since expanded to include women due to recessional contagion to other sectors where precarious and unstable labor relations prevail. Consequently, there is a gap in the unemployment rates of these groups (due to age, origin, or gender) with respect to percentages for the native adult male population, whose propensity to unemployment is generally much lower.

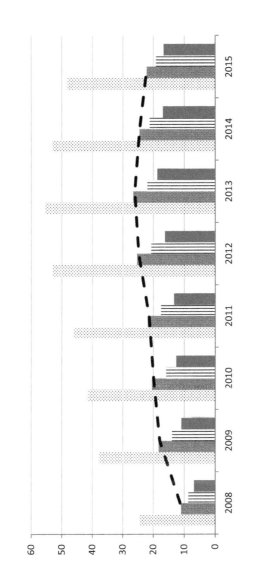

Figure 4.3 Unemployment rates by age, 2008–2015 (%)

Source: Own elaboration with data from Eurostat.

As seen in the previous section, temporality is one characteristic feature of the labor market that intensifies the difficulties caused by unemployment. Although its evolution has remained constant through recent decades, at around 30% to 35%, the non-renewal of temporary contracts since 2008 has made these jobs an instrument of adjustment, entailing minimal cost for companies in the readjustment of their models (Figure 4.4). Thus 90% of contracts created since 2008 have been temporary, and of these, an increasing percentage since the crisis began (between 19% and 27%) have been part-time (data from INE). Reversing the trend during the growth period, when permanent contracts used to outnumber temporary contracts when there was job creation, in 2014 and 2015 most of the new contracts (for both sexes) are temporary, exceeding the percentage that represents permanent employment in new contracts.

As with other problems affecting employment, temporary employment has had an unequal impact on employed persons overall. The decline in temporary employment at the onset of the crisis was greater in the case of men due to a greater male presence in sectors most affected by job loss (such as construction), the effect of which reduced the previously recorded gender gap. However, after 2010, recessionary consequences and the orientation of their management began to transfer problems to branches of activity where the proportion of women workers is higher, and this gap has resumed the growth path of recent years.

Part-time contracts, both indefinite and temporary, have become more prominent in the wake of the crisis (Figure 4.5). Before the crisis, the creation of part-time jobs had already begun to gain importance, even while full-time employment was rising, mainly among males. Total job creation during the early years of expansion was concentrated around women through part-time contracting. With the onset of the crisis, male employees experienced greater destruction of full-time employment, whereas overall part-time employment continued to see increases. In the case of women, it was not until 2009 that the hiring of full-time employees began to decline. This decrease continued until 2013, with the progressive effect of replacing full-time workers with part-time workers, the latter never having fallen, with the sole exception of 2007 for males (probably due to an economic slowdown that eliminated part-time male work created to cover the demand peaks of the bonanza stage).[15]

Although part-time contracts have been less relevant in Spain than in other EU economies of reference, their evolution tends to approach the EU aggregate. However, in contrast with other countries, part-time work does not tend to be a voluntary trend that favors the reconciliation of work and family life; rather, this relationship is overwhelmingly involuntary. At the beginning of the twenty-first century, the rate of involuntary participation in part-time contracts was around 20% in Spain. After the crisis began, that level rose to above 30%, and the latest available data for 2015 puts the figure at 63% (72% for men and 60% for women). This is very unlike the overall EU situation, which despite an upward trend showed a value of 29% for the same year.

It should be noted that the incidence of part-time contracts is much higher for women than for men. Of the total registered in Spain in 2015, 26% corresponded

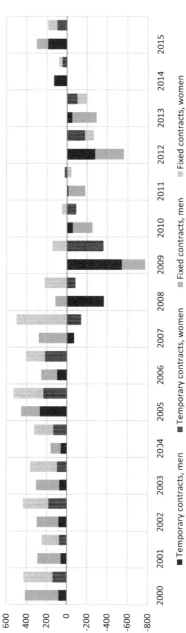

Figure 4.4 Annual change in the number of contracts (thousands)

Source: Own elaboration with data from Eurostat (Labor Force Survey).

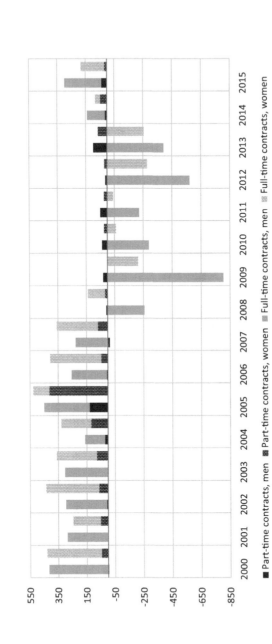

Figure 4.5 Annual change in part-time and full-time contracts (thousands)

Source: Own elaboration with data from Eurostat (Labor Force Survey).

to men and 74% to women. Also noteworthy is that increases in part-time contracts have not been proportionally voluntary in nature. The intention to work full time, resulting from the need to supplement household incomes in the face of the stagnation (or even decline) of real wages, along with the rise in family indebtedness in recent years, finds no satisfaction in the labor market, leading many to accept part-time contracts. At the same time, the transition of many women from market inactivity to an active job search means that a large segment has been able to reconcile a significant number of outside working hours with the responsibilities they maintain at home (housework and care work). This argument contradicts the idea that this type of employment is preferred in order to have more spare time.[16]

A final effect of the crisis is the wage share of GDP, which (as we will see in Figure 5.4 of the following chapter) has sharpened its downward trend since 2008 due to adjustments and internal devaluation leading to the loss of purchasing power.

Law reforms in the process of labor deregulation

As we have seen, all labor reforms and related decrees have been part of a long process that is structural in character, but it is worthwhile to highlight the impact of the three most recent reforms implemented in response to the current crisis. Since May 2010, austerity strategies with significant changes in wage relations have been promoted (Pérez Infante, 2013). The three labor reforms (LRs) implemented during the crisis (in 2010 and 2011 by the governing Socialist Party [PSOE] and in 2012 by the PP) reflect to varying degrees the strong process of flexibilization of labor relations and the lack of consensus among social agents (because none were signed by the major unions).

The LR of 2010 loosened the ban on 'austerity policy' packages that national and EU institutions had imposed as the only way to remedy the devastating effects of the crisis. In this case, the PSOE enacted a legislative reform with the purpose of activating measures that would serve to foster internal and external flexibility. On the one hand, this introduced mechanisms to speed the internal mobility of workers and the possibility of temporary suspensions of contractual relations. Data from the MESS show that collective dismissals (Expedientes de Regulación de Empleo or ERE, in Spanish) numbered 426,954 for suspension, 98,906 for extinction, and 120,515 for reduction between 2010 and 2011. Likewise, this reform raised the possibility for business to opt out from wage agreements. Regarding external flexibilization, the LR of 2010 declared its intention to end the duality between permanent and temporary contracts. To do so, it limited the duration of temporary contracts to three to four years, depending on the agreement, and it encouraged for all agreements the promotion of the type of indefinite contracts that were created in 1997, a modality that carried lower dismissal compensation than ordinary indefinite contracts.

Another measure taken was a reduction in the cost of dismissal and co-financing of the Wage Guarantee Fund, without redefining the causes and reasons for dismissal. In this regard, the reform opened the possibility of firing and justifying a collective dismissal (for more than 10% of the workforce) if a company declared negative results that jeopardized the viability of its activity. Likewise, the period of notice of termination of a contract was reduced from 30 to 15 days.

Along this same adjustment path, the main purpose of the LR of 2011 was to reconfigure the rules and fundamentals of collective bargaining. The essential changes were based on prioritizing the application of company agreements over all others and on maintaining ultra-activity (the extension of an agreement after it has been finalized), although with certain changes in cases where no agreement was reached.[17] At the same time, additional internal flexibilization measures were included in terms of working hours, temporary periods, and reference periods for the functional mobility of workers.

Despite union opposition to these legislative reforms, in early 2012 the Second Agreement for Employment and Collective Bargaining for 2012–2014 was signed by the main trade union confederations and by the employer associations. The public objective was to seek agreement on the scope of collective bargaining without the need for legal reforms. By intensifying internal flexibility, companies could cope with short-term problems without resorting to layoffs as an adjustment mechanism through a policy of moderating all incomes. Likewise, they declared the need to reinvest any surplus obtained to be used as a catalyst to improve the competitiveness of companies and thus generate employment.

Far from reaching such objectives, the LR of 2012 was approved by law a few months after the initial agreement. This law was the most forceful of the reforms and had greater effects on the structure of labor relations, especially in terms of collective bargaining. In terms of external flexibility, which is to say entry and exit of labor, different mechanisms were designed to speed the insertion of workers into the labor market and to reduce the number of workers leaving it. In this regard, a new type of contractual form (so-called 'entrepreneurial contract') was designed as a mechanism to allegedly encourage indefinite contracting by companies with fewer than 50 employees. During the first year of the contract, a company was permitted to dismiss an employee without cause or cost if the national unemployment rate was higher than 15%. Once the trial period was complete, an indefinite contractual relationship would be established.

Another way to make the mechanisms of entry more flexible was the introduction of the possibility of offering training and learning contracts to young workers under 30 years of age. Also permissible were overtime hours, in addition to existing part-time supplementary hours. Since these changes were introduced, training jobs and trainees have gained prominence in the labor market. All these mechanisms have served to increase precariousness and contractual vulnerability, with concurrent grim effects on future pensions and other labor rights.

In terms of dismissal, the new measures were even more forceful. Among the most striking was the reduction of severance payments from 45 to 33 days per year worked, with a maximum of 24 monthly payments. An additional method of reducing exit costs was to eliminate the processing of wages in cases of unfair dismissals after the first year of the contract.

Regarding collective dismissals, several relevant facets marked a turning point in their handling. In the first place, the need for administrative authorization was removed, leaving the decision open. Similarly, the acceptable causes for dismissal (especially economic ones) were amplified, to be based merely on decreases in revenue or sales. The impact of these measures is shown in Figure 4.6.

Concerning internal flexibility, many legislative measures were introduced in terms of wages, work time, and mobility, allowing the workforce to adapt to the needs of the company. One of the most radical in terms of collective bargaining was non-application of or non-compliance with the agreement. Also, a path of uni-lateral resolution by the employer was opened in case of conflicts where no agreement was reached; together with the priority of an employer's application over other agreements, this served to consolidate the necessary mechanisms to grant the employer greater power. Data from the latest Labor Force Surveys of 2013 and 2014 show that 49% of companies acknowledge that they have implemented some of these flexibilization measures introduced in the legislative reforms, the most applied measure being the elimination of jobs.

It is clear that because of these reforms, and especially those of 2012, a profound change has been made in the nature of the Workers' Statute and the relations between capital and labor. Moreover, these reforms have failed to achieve the job creation targets proposed. Indeed, the results obtained show strong job destruction, as well as strong increases in the precariousness of labor relations in terms of wages, working time, and contractual forms and conditions. Although wage devaluation was not among the explicitly stated objectives in the reforms, it has in fact been an implicit element, reflected in the reduced purchasing power of the working class.

Wage devaluation as a strategy against the crisis

Crisis management has been marked by internal devaluation policies as the chief strategy to achieve gains in external competitiveness. Spain is a member of the Eurozone, which prevents external devaluation of the nominal exchange rate as a way of reducing the prices of exports, compared to competitors. The trade and productive imbalances typical of dynamics within the monetary zone, as discussed in Chapter 2, place deficit countries in a difficult and complex position. The guide-lines of the Bank of Spain and international economic institutions (such as the European Central Bank, the European Commission, and the International Monetary Fund) recommend wage devaluation as the best way to improve competitiveness and to create jobs. In the context of conventional economic theories, wage moderation and reduction should reduce unit labor costs, thus improving competitiveness. In this way, balance of trade should be achieved through an increase in exports, and all of this would result in a set of positive productive and commercial effects that would in turn spur the creation of employment (Pérez Infante, 2013).

One way to verify the effectiveness of the application of wage devaluation strategies and policies in the Spanish economy is through the rate of change experienced in wage costs. As shown in Figure 4.7, the evolution of wage costs since

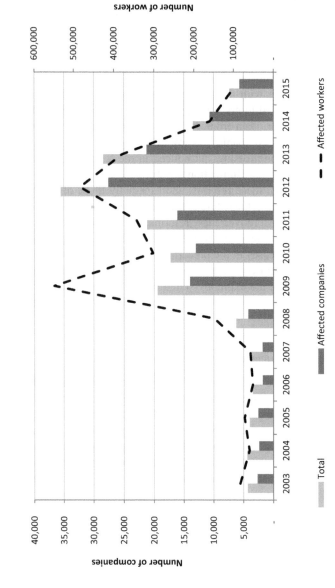

Figure 4.6 Collective dismissals (EREs), number of companies, and workers affected, 2003–2015

Source: Own elaboration with data from MESS.

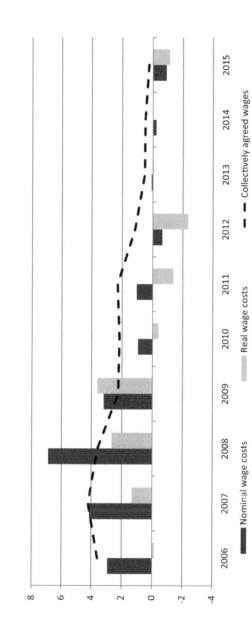

Figure 4.7 Gross wages, 2006–2014 (annual growth rates)

Source: Own elaboration with data from INE and MESS.

2010 displays a sharp drop compared to the previous year, reaching negative rates in real terms. This trend worsens in subsequent years, especially in 2012, obtaining a cumulative reduction of more than 7% between 2010 and 2014. If we analyze the evolution of agreed wages, we find a decreasing trend since 2009, sharpened by the agreements reached in 2012, 2013, and 2014. We also confirm that not only have the agreed-upon wage rises not been met, but between 2012 and 2014 nominal wages were either frozen or reduced.

Drawing nominal average wage data from the INE's Labor Force Survey, we observe how the rates of change from 2009 to 2014 reflect wage moderation and the loss of purchasing power over the crisis period. It is important to highlight the loss of purchasing power amounting to over 9% for part-time contracts and of 12% for temporary part-time contracts, which is a concern, given the increase in these contractual forms (in particular when involuntary).

Linked with all these factors, as another result of the process of transformation of labor relations in Spain, the category of the 'working poor'[18] has strongly emerged (which illustrates the poor quality of many new jobs created). According to Eurostat, in 2015 about 15% of wage earners in Spain were at risk of poverty. The proportion of workers at risk of poverty has risen sharply since 2004 in the cases of younger workers (from 8.4% to 21.3%), workers with a part-time contract (from 16% to 22.9%), workers with a temporary contract (from 13% to 22%), and the self-employed (currently at more than 26%). Another alarming consequence of this crisis is that in more than 1,700,000 households all family members of working age are unemployed. The greatest increase has been in populations of unemployed persons who since the crisis have withdrawn from the job market and who suffer a low possibility of reentry.

In addition to the role that wages play in the economy (representing a cost to companies and being key to aggregate demand), they reflect the interrelations between labor and capital and constitute the main source of income for the population. The results presented here corroborate a clear process of internal devaluation as a response to the crisis, the main strategy to facilitate the recovery of capital profitability, and that explains the unequal burden when sharing the costs of the crisis, as shown in Chapter 5.

Conclusions

Throughout this chapter we have analyzed the structural and current factors that have characterized the Spanish labor market, with special emphasis on the current crisis period. From our analysis, it is possible to draw the following conclusions.

Over recent decades a process of deregulation of labor relations has taken place, a process of structural change that has allowed for the application of policies and business strategies which have come to normalize the precariousness of employment in Spain. Also significant have been the impacts on contractual temporality and wage stagnation (due to a growth model that has prevented substantial improvements in productivity, as discussed in Chapter 1), and this has meant a constant deterioration in labor conditions and in the labor share of national income. As we will see in the next chapter, this has had relevant consequences for the evolution of income inequality.

It is evident that changes in the world of work, including individualization and the emergence of new identities among workers, together with flexible strategies and policies, have led to a complex labor panorama. The intensification of labor segmentation and the polarization between different groups of workers have been increasing through recent decades. Although those most affected in the recession years have been employees in the most fragile and vulnerable segments of the market, the labor policies applied have not only increased their precariousness but have normalized and extended insecurity for other groups of workers.

All this has fomented a scenario of dismantled bargaining and collective action practices that not only affect the worker as an individual and increase the inequality between workers, but also represents a clear attack on trade union organizations. The weakening and disempowerment of trade union representation have disrupted collective action as well as bargaining strategies, which has in turn put distance between the unions and the most vulnerable and precarious groups. Several factors undoubtedly explain the deterioration of collective bargaining – some linked to external changes in the productive model, others to the policies and legislative reforms that have transformed the labor relations framework – but the major unions have also been party to the causes and consequences of these changes in the correlation of forces between capital and labor.

Stability, permanent employment, the reduction of working hours, and other rights and conditions that many once enjoyed have been replaced by higher levels of temporality, partiality, greater intensity in work pace, and, ultimately, greater pressures for a large part of the working class. After the difficult period of job destruction faced in the early years of the crisis, the new contracts offer lower wages, poorer conditions, and degraded rights – in general, lower levels of protection of living conditions for the overall population. Inequality in labor conditions and rights, as well as the costs of flexibilization, indicate the normalization and institutionalization of precariousness in the labor market, and a transfer of risks and costs to the working class that has extended, alarmingly, to those who still have good and stable jobs.

Clearly, the precariousness of labor relations has a structural character and a long-term trajectory. However, with the outbreak of the current crisis, we have come to see that many of the costs deriving from the process of labor deregulation and policies of wage devaluation have placed an increasing number of people in a position of extreme insecurity in terms of poverty and exclusion. On the other hand, the objectives that such changes were meant to pursue, especially the improvement of external competitiveness (as described in Chapter 2), have thus far not been achieved.

Reversing this situation would mean abandoning the guidelines that have shaped the labor reforms of recent years and reversing occupational policies that have only weakened trade union power, dismantled social dialogue and social agreement, and preserved few protective mechanisms for working conditions under the argument of flexibility, instead making strong use of indiscriminate dismissal and precariousness to transfer market risks to employment through adjustments.

Moving beyond those elements that have degraded the labor market in recent years, we are aware of the need to apply restructuring measures to the production model of the Spanish economy which, in the short and medium terms, could help to alleviate some tensions in the labor market. In this sense, potential transformations that might bring us closer to other EU scenarios (not without difficulties, but with job opportunities that would surpass those offered in Spain) must, on the one hand, reorient the labor-intensive sectors towards greater quality and innovation and, on the other hand, promote those branches of activity that generate jobs with good hiring conditions. In this way, gains in competitiveness would not focus on labor costs but rather on the continuous improvement of other elements, including innovation and quality, higher technological content, or progress towards sustainability and the greater efficiency of processes.

Of course, in order to ensure that these productive improvements are transferred into job opportunities and improved working conditions, institutional will and pressure by workers and their representatives will be necessary to revive prior mechanisms of control and to safeguard against the propagation of flexibility formulas as a tool to increase business profits. It will be further necessary to develop a new legislative framework that can contribute to controlling and limiting business strategies based on obtaining greater profitability at the cost of labor and the intensification of work. Labor reform is needed that defends the rights of workers to combat the segmentation and polarization of the working class, thus recovering the strength and functionality that collective bargaining enjoyed when the Workers' Statute was initially signed.

Notes

1 Author names are given in alphabetical order, as both share equal responsibility for this chapter.
2 In this sense, flexibility was the response to this supposed 'rigidity' by fitting the changes in the economic relations of the new scenario with the labor markets of the European economies (Boyer, 1986).
3 Whereas in some European countries labor flexibility was combined with a reinforcement of coverage and levels of social protection ('flexicurity' applied in the Nordic countries), in others such as Spain, flexibility basically adjusted the quantity and characteristics of employment to the changing requirements of markets.
4 Some examples of 'rigidities' were the establishment of a minimum wage, state regulation in the labor market, entry and exit costs, social contributions, and union power.
5 We use this concept from the definitions of conventional economics in the assumptions of macroeconomic equilibrium, referring to distorting variables that prevent the perfect equilibrium between markets. Authors such as Pérez Infante (2013) further develop these definitions of conventional economics.
6 As for the conditions, it should be noted that the agricultural sector showed a distance from the national average temporality rate of more than 25 points, being at around 30% at the turn of the century and 25% in the early years of the crisis (following the strong impact of unemployment on contingent contracts). Something similar, although with less emphasis, occurs in construction, which has always been above 35%; still

more distant but above average are low-skilled services. These are also the sectors at the lower end of the wage scale, and their evolution has been less favorable than with other activities: the industrial sector and skilled services saw real wages reduced in the process of devaluation between 1995 and 2007, but not so strongly as in construction or non-skilled services. When the recession began and real wages were increased by recessive effects, variations in these sectors of employment still showed negative rates of change in some branches of non-skilled services (as in the hotel industry, among others).

7 We understand labor deregulation as a broad process that goes beyond legislative reforms and combines a set of policies that not only adapt the labor market to the needs of capital, but also represent a significant change in the correlation of forces in the processes of negotiation between capital and labor (Ruesga et al., 2005).

8 The degree of reform has been different, and some reforms were not as deregulatory as that of 2002. On the other hand, the most striking reforms and those that had the greatest impact were the Labor Reform of 1984 (with the opening of the labor framework towards temporality), that of 1994 (with the creation of Temporary Employment Agencies [TEA]), and finally that of 2012 (which modified the basis of collective bargaining).

9 Although it is not the object of this study to address what has happened to the set of variables that indicate all sources of income of the population (wages, but also pensions or unemployment benefits in their different modalities or other incomes linked to social protection), the fact is that the process of flexibility in Spain has generated greater fragility in the social protection system and has progressively limited and diminished the redistributive role of national government. See also the next chapter.

10 In other developed countries, the application of the Toyotian strategies of 'just in time' or 'lean production' began in the 1970s in the aftermath of the crisis of Fordism. In Spain, however, these organizational methods were introduced years later. For more information, see De la Garza (1999), Neffa (1999) and Boyer and Freyssenet (2003).

11 The indicators on employment and working conditions show a continuity of the precariousness of labor relations, with little change in their evolution and with truly alarming data on unemployment and temporary employment rates, both above the EU average.

12 The Spanish union affiliation rate remains the second lowest in the EU-15 after France, contrasting with countries such as Sweden, Finland, and Denmark (at around 75% to 80%).

13 Despite the increasing presence of women delegates and young representatives, there are still strong differences with respect to men over the age of 40.

14 Data obtained from the Labor Quality of Life Surveys of the MESS.

15 Although pre-crisis data show that full-time hiring in Spain was at 92% in 2000 and 88% in 2007, the decline has continued, to 83% of the total in 2015, with a concurrent rise in partial contracts, which amounted to 12% in that same year.

16 When having to choose between a part-time or a full-time job, the former is chosen when differences in income, rights, and working conditions do not differ to a significant degree. However, Spain gives a clear example that, despite all the limitations that may arise in conciliation issues (family, studies, or other uses of time), the divergence is such that most employees with part-time work contracts have simply not found a full-time job.

17 In cases of not reaching a new agreement in the maximum term of a negotiation, the procedures of either national or regional inter-professional agreements should be applied, including the arbitration process. This process becomes mandatory with this LR, although the aforementioned inter-professional agreements did not establish procedures to resolve discrepancies.

18 This category accounts for those individuals who, despite being employed, have a level of income below 60% of the national average, thus depriving them of an acceptable standard of living.

122   *M. Eugenia Ruiz-Gálvez and Lucía Vicent*

References

Baylos, A.P. (2014): 'Cambios en el mundo del trabajo', *Informes Fundación 1 de Mayo*, 89.

Blanco, J.B. (2004): 'El sindicalismo español frente a las nuevas estrategias empresariales de trabajo y empleo', *Cuadernos de relaciones laborales*, 22 (2), pp. 93–115.

Boyer, R. (1986): *La flexibilidad del trabajo en Europa: un estudio comparativo de las transformaciones del trabajo asalariado en siete países entre 1973 y 1985*, Madrid: Ministerio de Trabajo y Seguridad Social.

Boyer, R. and Freyssenet, M. (2003): *Los modelos productivos*, Madrid: Editorial Fundamentos.

Castillo, J.J. (2005): *El trabajo recobrado. Una evaluación del trabajo realmente existente en España*, Buenos Aires-Madrid: Miño y Dávila.

Castillo, J.J. and López Calle, P. (2009): 'Modelos productivos, salud laboral y políticas de prevención: el caso español', *Revista La Mutua*, 21, segunda época, pp. 77–97.

De la Garza Toledo, E. (1999): 'Epistemología de las teorías sobre modelos de producción', in E. De la Garza Toledo (comp.), *Los retos teóricos de los estudios del trabajo hacia el siglo XXI*, Buenos Aires: CLACSO (Consejo Latinoamericano de las Ciencias Sociales).

De Serres, A., Scarpetta, S. and De la Maisonneuve, C. (2001): 'Falling Wage Shares in Europe and the United States: How Important Is Aggregation Bias?', *Empirica*, 28 (4), pp. 375–401.

Durand, J.P. (2011): *La cadena invisible: flujo tenso y servidumbre voluntaria*, México DF: Fondo de Cultura Económica, Universidad Autónoma Metropolitana.

Fina, Ll. (2001): *El reto del empleo*, Madrid: McGraw-Hill.

Fina, Ll. and Toharia, L. (1987), *Las causas del paro en España: un punto de vista estructural*, Madrid: Fundación IESA.

Gaffard, J.L. and Sarraceno, F. (2009): 'Redistribution des revenus et instabilité. À la recherche des causes réelles de la crise financière', *Revue de l'OFCE*, 110 (3), pp. 75–86.

González, S. and Guillén, M. (2009): 'La calidad del empleo en la Unión Europea: Debate político y construcción de indicadores', *Revista del Ministerio de Trabajo e Inmigración*, 81, pp. 71–88.

López, E. and Malo, M.A. (2015): 'El mercado de trabajo en España el contexto europeo, los dos viejos desafíos y un nuevo problema', *Ekonomiaz: Revista vasca de economía*, 87, pp. 32–59.

Miguélez, F. (1995): 'El mercado de trabajo en España y la persistencia de las diferencias con la Unión Europea: ¿Un modelo de expansión?', *Economía y sociología del trabajo*, 27–28, pp. 61–73.

Miguélez, F. and Prieto, C. (2009): 'Trasformaciones del empleo, flexibilidad y relaciones laborales en Europa', *Política y Sociedad*, 46, pp. 275–287.

Mingione, E. (1993): *Las sociedades fragmentadas*, Madrid: Ministerio de Trabajo y Seguridad Social.

Neffa, J.C. (1999): 'Actividad, trabajo y empleo: algunas reflexiones sobre un tema en debate', *Orientación y sociedad*, 1, pp. 127–161.

Pérez Infante, J. (2013): 'Crisis, reformas laborales y devaluación salarial', *Relaciones laborales: Revista crítica de teoría y práctica*, 10, pp. 69–96.

Piore, M. and Sabel, C. (1990): *La segunda ruptura industrial*, Madrid: Alianza.

Pitxer, J.V. and Sánchez, A. (2008): 'Estrategias sindicales y modelo económico español', *Cuadernos de Relaciones Laborales*, 26 (1), pp. 89–122.

Ruesga, S.M., Valdés, F. and Zulfiaur, J.M. (Coord.). (2005): *Transformaciones laborales en España: A XXV años de la promulgación del Estatuto de los Trabajadores*, Madrid: Ministerio de Trabajo y Asuntos Sociales.

Sola, J. (2010): 'La desregulación política del mercado de trabajo en España (1984–1997): Un programa de investigación', *Revista de economía crítica*, 9, pp. 4–30.

Sola, J. (2014): 'El legado histórico franquista y el mercado de trabajo en España', *RES. Revista Española de Sociología*, 21, pp. 99–128.

Streeck, W. (1988): 'Comment on "Rigidities in the Labour Market"', *Government and Opposition*, 23 (4), pp. 413–423.

5 The distributive pattern of the Spanish economy

The impact of adjustment on inequalities

Luis Buendía, Ricardo Molero-Simarro, and F. Javier Murillo Arroyo[1]

Introduction

Having understood the fundamental features of the process of accumulation before and through the crisis, in both its internal and external dimensions (Chapters 1, 2, and 3), and having examined the impact on the labor market of the overall process of growth, crisis, and adjustment, we now turn to the inequality of income, as prescribed in the book's Introduction. Our analysis will focus on the study of the main determinants of inequality in a capitalist economy: on the one hand, the distribution of wealth, and the functional distribution of national income among wages and profits; and, on the other hand, the redistributive impact of the state and the results in terms of personal inequality of income, monetary poverty, and social exclusion. The evolution of these variables has been greatly determined by the process of wage adjustment initiated in the final decades of the twentieth century.

Understanding wage adjustment as the global reaction adopted to cope with increasing tensions over the profitability of capital, as discussed in Chapter 1, we find that the rate of profitability deteriorated throughout the period under analysis and even during the growth phase. This has worsened since 2006, when the bulk of profits experienced an intense decline. In the face of that situation, attempts have been made to activate accumulation by promoting an income distribution favorable to corporate profits, toward which end a framework of wage containment has been comprehensively deployed, encompassing direct components (monetary earnings received by wage earners), indirect components (remuneration in kind obtained through the provision of public services by the state), and deferred components (various monetary transfers, including unemployment benefits and pensions).

In the European economies, this adjustment has been implemented within the framework of the European Union (EU), where the Single European Act and the adoption of the euro currency have shaped some of the main adjustment measures. The requirements of access to the single currency generated a scenario of fiscal and monetary discipline and exchange rate stability. Considering the framework of free capital mobility in the EU, fiscal austerity can be understood as being closely related to wage incomes, in particular in their deferred components (increased difficulty of access to the main public benefits) and indirect components (via privatizations). To this must be added wage moderation, analyzed in Chapter 4 and justified to contain price growth and promoting a process of internal deflation directed at workers' wages so as not to undermine profits (Del Rosal and Murillo, 2015).

The ongoing functioning of the Economic and Monetary Union (EMU) has ensured continuity in all these trends. Through various amendments to the Stability and Growth Pact, originally signed in 1997, and the so-called Euro Pact of 2011, the program of fiscal austerity has been kept in effect. In addition, the exchange rate policy was transferred from member states to the European Central Bank (ECB), adding to the pressure on wages in order to improve external competitiveness.

In the previous chapter, it was explained that the route to improve profitability taken during the overall period of analysis has been wage devaluation. In particular, before the outbreak of the current crisis, the need to improve competitiveness was defended through a focus on measures to contain unit labor costs (ULC), as seen in Chapters 2 and 4. Underlying this discourse is the basic distributive conflict of capitalist economies which takes place between capital and labor. In the case of the peripheral economies of the EMU, where productivity had made only modest advances (Chapter 1), a reduction in ULC has been achieved at the cost of deep wage regression.

In short, the path maintained by income distribution has responded to intense wage adjustment, applied with the goal of counteracting growing tensions over the profitability of capital. This adjustment has occurred on a global scale, although in the case of the Spanish economy it has been mediated by its integration into the EMU in a context of welfare state underdevelopment. In addition, Spain's economy features a series of peculiarities, among which its low technical profile may be highlighted (Chapters 1 and 2).

Although wage adjustment began to be implemented during the expansion phase (1995–2007), it was intensified during the recession phase (2007–2015), moving us to structure this chapter into four sections. This brief introduction is followed by an analysis of the evolution of income distribution in the pre-crisis period, focusing on five main factors: functional income distribution, wage dispersion, concentration of wealth, the evolution of earnings, and the role of the state in terms of taxes and transfers. In the third section, we examine these variables since the outbreak of the crisis, as well as their effect on the Gini Index, monetary poverty, material deprivation, and social exclusion. Finally, the fourth section presents our main conclusions.

Distribution of income during the period of growth

The varied set of measures that have shaped the process of wage adjustment, along with the real estate bias of Spain's economic growth, has had direct consequences on the inequality of income and on poverty.

Distribution of wealth and primary income inequality

To understand the effects of the crisis on inequality, we begin by considering primary income inequality; that is, the inequality generated in the productive sphere before the redistributive involvement of the state, allowing us to observe how the conditions of wage adjustment (in which impressive growth was cemented) prevented the generation of jobs that would translate into substantial improvements in overall living conditions.

Wealth distribution

The study of the structure of ownership of the means of production ultimately determines the pattern of income distribution and enables understanding of the dynamics of the Spanish social structure itself. In addition, it enables the determination of whether workers, as a class, have participated in the equity gains linked to speculative bubbles and whether wage moderation has been offset by the greater participation of workers in income derived from ownership of assets. The Survey of Household Finances (in Spanish, Encuesta Financiera de las Familias or EFF) has been used to inform this study.[2]

Figure 5.1 reflects the participation of workers in real estate ownership.[3] Specifically, for each of the assets analyzed, we have calculated the percentage representing the value of assets held by workers in relation to the total value of each.[4] In the case of the main residence, no significant differences were observed when comparing participation in gross and net terms, and only a slightly smaller participation is revealed when the value of debt is deducted. Despite this being the asset where the participation of workers is highest, because of the high incidence of ownership of the primary residence in Spain, wage earners maintain a percentage of property inferior to that corresponding to their relative weight in the social structure as a consequence of the differences in value between houses owned. That is to say, the differences between social classes do not correspond so much to unequal access to property, but rather to the differences in the average values of the residences owned. Nevertheless, in both cases, regarding the value of this asset in gross or net terms, the share of workers in residential ownership has been decreasing.

In the case of all other real estate, the proportion owned by wage earners is lower than that of the main residence. Although only a small part of these assets is used as a means of production, their inclusion in this analysis allows assessment of who may benefit from equity gains linked to the real estate bubble. Only a small percentage of these assets (21.3% in net terms in 2008) showing a fractional decrease (from 23.9% in 2002) remained in the hands of the working class, meaning that their potential capital gains were residual.

More important is the analysis of the distribution of ownership of financial assets, also subject to their own speculative bubble, which is shown in Figure 5.2. In 2002, the share of workers in the value of stock and other ownership titles

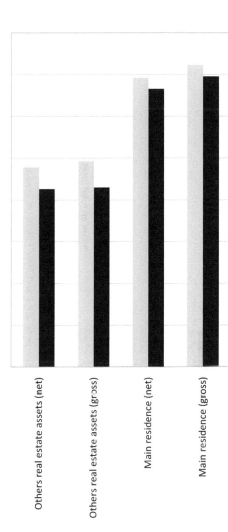

Figure 5.1 Real estate assets owned by wage earners, 2002 and 2008 (share on total asset value)
Source: Own elaboration with data from BoS (EFF).

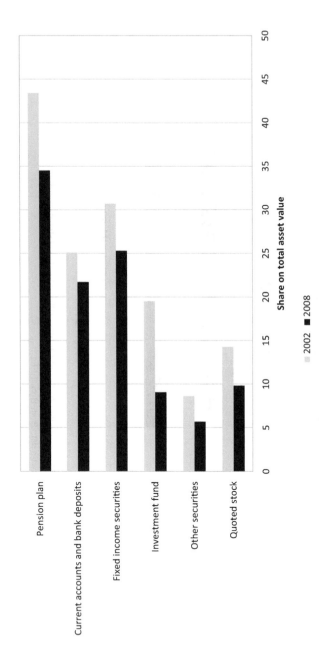

Figure 5.2 Financial assets owned by wage earners, 2002 and 2008 (share on total asset value)

Source: Own elaboration with data from BoS (EFF).

was marginal (at 14.3% and 8.6%, respectively). During the final years of the so-called Spanish miracle, these shares were reduced in both cases (down to 9.8% and 5.7%, respectively). Thus, it becomes clear that the growth pattern boosted the asymmetric distribution of the means of production.

Other assets representing ownership of the means of production are investment funds and pension funds.[5] Again, there was a decline in the value of the property of employees throughout the period, especially outstanding in the case of invest-ment funds, where ownership by workers fell by half. In this regard, such assets have not served to promote the participation of employees in the ownership of the means of production. The relative weight of workers in terms of property is higher in the case of pension schemes, to a certain extent because individual plans and retirement insurance are both included, as are employment-based plans. In addition, ownership of these assets is more widespread among wage earners as a consequence of the deterioration of the public system, explaining their greater propensity to direct their savings towards these assets. Also, in the case of fixed-income financial assets and in liquid and deposit accounts, the shares held by workers fell across the period.

Therefore, far from favoring wider extension of ownership of the means of pro-duction, the dynamics of accumulation experienced during the pre-crisis growth phase generated a more concentrated ownership structure. This process is the underside of the increasing share of wage earners in the active population. The result has been an increasingly polarized social structure, with a growing propor-tion of society whose main source of income is wages, which have themselves been subject to constriction throughout the period, while a minority of the popula-tion has concentrated more property. Analysis of the participation of workers in the ownership of various assets makes possible the demystification of the idea that privatizations and deregulation policies promote the spreading of wealth across different social classes.

Capital gains and top incomes

Given this deterioration in the distribution of wealth, it is no surprise that the capi-tal gains made possible by the housing bubble favored mainly those families and individuals with higher incomes.[6] The income shares held by the top 10%, 5%, and 1% of the richest persons in terms of gross income increased significantly. For the top 10%, this figure rose from 33.6% in 1993 to 34.7% in 2007; for the top 5% over the same period, from 22.1% to 24.2% (down slightly from 25.9% in 2006); and in the case of the richest 1%, from 5.4% to 8.2%.[7] In terms of the significance of the other income components (and capital gains) for wealthier individuals, the relevance of wealth distribution is again confirmed. Labor income, entrepreneur-ial income, and capital income decreased their shares among the top 10%, 5%, and 1% of richest persons pre-tax income. At the same time, capital gains rose to 19.1% for the richest 10% in 2006, to 25.3% for the richest 5%, and to 42.5% for the top 1% of individuals (Figure 5.3).[8]

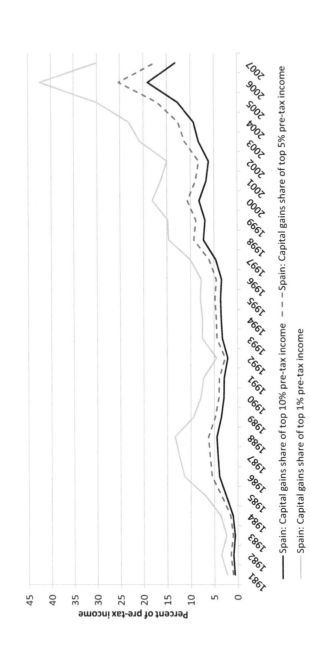

Figure 5.3 Capital gains share in top incomes, 1981–2007

Note: The relevance of capital gains is calculated as the share of capital gains in pre-tax income of top income households according to personal income tax data.

Source: Own elaboration with data from the World Top Incomes Database.

Wage dynamics

Next, the pattern of income distribution is analyzed from a functional perspective, which is of great relevance given the prioritization of capital needs in the pattern of accumulation in Spain.[9] Figure 5.4 shows the evolution of the main indicators linked with the functional perspective through the period of analysis, revealing two clear trends: the relative profit (or Profit Share) has grown throughout the period (interrupted only by the crisis), rising from 34.2% to 37.1% during the growth phase, whereas the relative wage (or Wage Share) stagnated, reaching 53.7% in 2007 from an earlier 53.2%.

Nonetheless, it is impossible to understand the magnitude of the regression that wages have undergone without taking into account a major change in the Spanish social structure during recent decades: the increasing share of salaried workers in the whole population, or 'salarization'. According to Labor Force Survey data, the relative weight of wage earners, employed and unemployed, in the total work-force rose from 80.7% in 1996 to 83.8% in 2007. This does not mean that none abandoned this social class in favor of others, but rather that the predominant flow was from other classes to the working class. This process is particularly notewor-thy in sectors such as hospitality and retail trade, given the productive structure of Spanish capitalism.

However, the erosion of the wage share is compatible with an increase in aver-age real wages, as long as productivity grows at a faster rate than wages. In the case of Spain, the low technical profile of its productive dynamic and its orienta-tion towards branches less exposed to technical change have determined minimal progress in terms of productivity, as was pointed out in Chapter 1. In this context, the trajectory maintained by the wage share has been the main consequence of the subjugation of salaries. In average terms, despite a process of economic growth in Spain superior to that of the main economic powers, real wages experienced a regression that caused them to decline over the period. Specifically, average real wages fell between 3% and 4% over the period 1996–2007, depending on whether they are expressed in terms of the number of hours worked or the number of full-time employees.[10]

Therefore, the combination of the path followed by the wage share and the increasing relative weight of wage earners in the active population allows a more precise view of the impact of economic growth on the salaried class during the period, with a clear involution of wages resulting from the needs of capital to revive accumulation.

Wage dispersion

According to our analysis of the available data sources, it seems implausible to attribute the increase in inequality during this phase to wage disparities. Analysis of State Agency of Tax Administration (AEAT, according to its Spanish acronym) data reflects lower dispersion in salary distribution: the upper category (workers with a wage of at least quadruple the minimum wage, or SMI in Spanish) and lower category (workers with a wage less than half the SMI) both lost relative importance at the expense of the intermediate category (Figure 5.5). However,

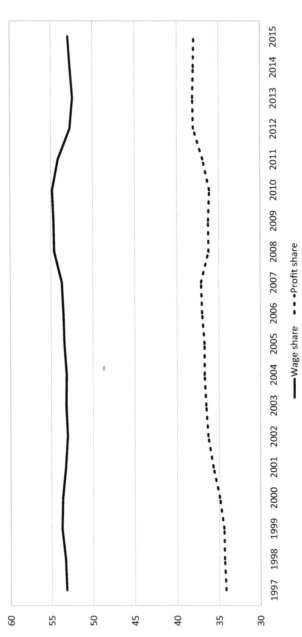

Figure 5.4 Functional income distribution, 1997–2015 (% of GDP$_{fc}$)

Source: Own elaboration with data from INE and AMECO.

Wage share   • • • Profit share

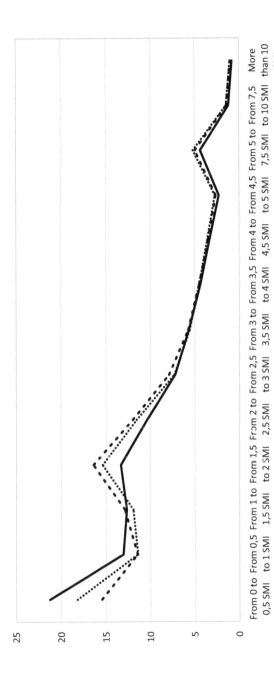

Figure 5.5 Wage earners by salary level according to the SMI, 2000, 2007, and 2015 (%)

Source: Own elaboration with data from AEAT.

workers who earned a maximum wage double the SMI maintained their relative weight with respect to the total, at around 56%. In this regard, everything indicates that wage adjustment did not lead to a rebound in wage dispersion, but that the distributive conflict between capital and labor was responsible for increasing inequality.

Although it could be argued that wage containment has only affected the new jobs created, if we complement our analysis with wage dispersion ratios offered by the Organisation for Economic Co-operation and Development (OECD), it can be confirmed that adjustment has permeated the various salary scales. Table 5.1 shows that wage differentials were attenuated over the period so that downward pressure from wage adjustment affected wage earners as a whole, even if the lower strata felt this pressure with more intensity. This is the case with the female labor force, which has been subjected to greater precariousness: according to Eurostat data, the unadjusted gender pay gap reached 18.1% in 2007.

Primary income inequality

Overall, despite the containment of wage dispersion, the evolution of the average real wage caused the percentage of workers at risk of poverty to decline only slightly, from 10.8% to 10.2% between 2004 (the first year of Eurostat data) and 2007, maintaining a percentage significantly higher than the EU-15 average, at 7.9% in 2007. In addition, the working class saw no compensation for the downward pressure on wages through a growing share of income derived from property. Nor were they the main beneficiaries of potential capital gains from the housing bubble. Not surprisingly, the high levels of inequality in the distribution of wealth increased over the period as the share of workers in the ownership of primary assets deteriorated.

Only thanks to job creation were inequality and pre-tax poverty reduced. According to Eurostat data, the Gini Index before social transfers (pensions included in social transfers) decreased from 47.7 to 43.4 points between 2004 and 2007. Meanwhile, poverty before social transfers (measured from an income threshold of 60% of median) fell from 42.1% to 38.7% of the population between 2004 and 2007. However, as we shall see, during the period of growth the foundations were laid for deepening the recent wage adjustments.

Table 5.1 Wage dispersion ratios, 1995–2014

	1995	2007	2014
Ratio Deciles 9/1	4.22	3.47	3.08
Ratio Deciles 9/5	2.1	2.06	1.88
Ratio Deciles 5/1	2.01	1.68	1.64

Source: Own elaboration with data from OECD.

Redistribution of the public sector and secondary income inequality

The redistributive capacity of the public sector

The idea of social underdevelopment in Spain, as presented by Navarro (2006), is reflected in two aspects that must be differentiated. On the one hand, there is the *effort*, which is the expenditures made on social aspects by the public sector. On the other hand, are the *results* of that effort, which influence the effectiveness of the Spanish welfare state (WS) in the performance of its functions. Measuring effort as social spending, between 1996 and 2008, this remained at around 20% of GDP, fluctuating up or down by 1 percentage point, which demonstrates that the fruits of extraordinary economic growth were not used to improve the WS, at least in quantitative terms.[11] The same figure for the EU-15 was around 26% for the same period. However, by measuring social expenditure in constant euros per capita, Spain's spending, which was 54% of the EU-15 average, increased to reach 61% in 2008 (Eurostat data).

Evidently, although this last indicator does show an increase in the effort put forth, the earlier indicator shows that, in light of the growth experienced by the economy, it would have been possible to attempt to reduce the gap that justifies categorization of Spain's WS as underdeveloped. This becomes even more evident in Figure 5.6, which shows that Spain's social effort has been lower than what would correspond to its level of development (approximated by GDP per capita in purchasing power parity, or PPP). Thus, whereas Portugal or Italy came closer in their effort to their respective levels of development (closer to the trend line), Spain, like Ireland, remains far from that mark (and Denmark presents the exact opposite case).

Using Eurostat data to assess WS results, we have calculated the redistributive capacity of the WS from both inequality and at-risk-of-poverty rates.[12] In the final years of the expansionary period, the WS in Spain went from reducing 35% of inequality to just 25%, whereas in the EU-15, there was a stagnation at around 38% (the arithmetic average). In terms of poverty risk, the reduction due to social transfers was also attenuated over the expansion phase, from 56.1% in 1996 to 47.6% in 2008 (when the EU-15 figure was at 62.3%). Focusing on this latter indicator, Figure 5.7 shows that at the end of the expansionary period, Spain showed levels far below what would correspond to its level of development, it being the country with the lowest redistributive capacity of the sample.

We complete this assessment with another factor: the institutional nature of the Spanish WS. This has been characterized as a hybrid between the different regimes existing in Europe, with traces of the others depending on the component we observe (Rodríguez Cabrero, 2011; Moreno, 2001). The result renders a Mediterranean-type WS, whose main features would be its scant redistributive capacity, its bias favoring the elderly over children and youth, and its high risk of poverty, as indicated by Gutiérrez (2014).

The reforms introduced during the expansion phase deepened the liberal features of the model, a trend that helps illuminate its quantitative evolution. Within

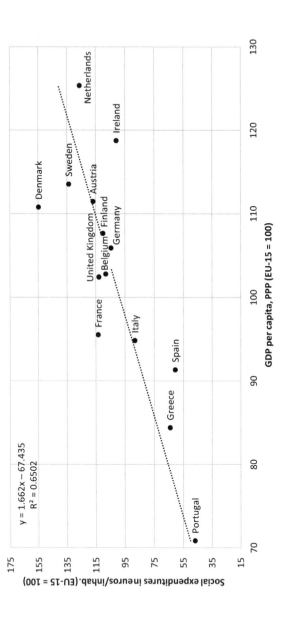

Figure 5.6 Economic development and social effort in the EU, 2008

Note: We have chosen all EU-15 countries except Luxembourg, which is an outlier given its extreme values.

Source: Own elaboration with data from Eurostat.

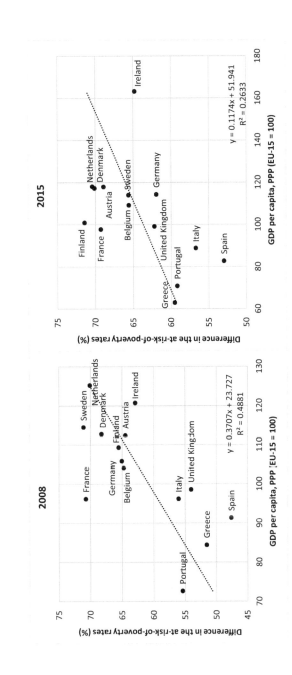

Figure 5.7 Redistributive capacity in EU-15 welfare states, 2008 and 2015

Note: The redistributive capacity is calculated as the difference in percentage of the at-risk-of-poverty rates before and after social transfers (cut-off point: 60% of median equalized income). See also our Note in Figure 5.6.

Source: Own elaboration with data from Eurostat.

these reforms, one could highlight the outsourcing of services (through selective privatization, for example) or the worsening of certain monetary benefits (to encourage activation of the population). Only in the latter part of the expansionary period did trends tend to compensate for some liberalizing components with the expansion of other aspects (albeit to a limited extent), as in the case of long-term care (through the so-called Dependency Law) or work/life balance (see Leon and Pavolini, 2014; Muñoz de Bustillo and Antón, 2015; Rodríguez Cabrero, 2011).

In addition to this was the fiscal reorganization deployed during this phase. The inheritance tax was eliminated and other figures were reformed. Personal income tax became less progressive by establishing a single rate for income derived from savings, independent of and lower than the tax levied on labor income, as well as by narrowing the maximum and minimum rates (the maximum was reduced by 23.2% between 1994 and 2007). The general corporation tax rate was reduced from 35% to 30%, although the effective rate has been much lower due to a range of tax deductions. Finally, capital enjoys various avenues by which to elude and evade its fiscal obligations (creation of holding companies, SICAV, etc.). All of this has occurred in a scenario of fiscal discipline.

Regarding the treatment of gender inequality, an improvement in pre-school education institutions since the 1990s has meant that the school attendance rate for ages 3 to 6 years reached practically 100% (even when voluntary). By contrast, in the age range of 0 to 3 years, the picture was very different, where the recourse to private providers meant the deterioration of working conditions of those people employed in such services. On the other hand, measures were introduced for a better work/life balance, including monetary support for working mothers (1,200 euros per child per year) and subsidies to companies employing women. In the last part of the expansionary phase, these measures, which were not reversed, were complemented by others of a more legislative nature, with the creation of official bodies specifically responsible for gender issues (including a ministry).

Likewise, the maternity and paternity benefits were improved and the Dependency Law for long-term care was introduced. However, inadequate funding (for both measures) and the terms of this law meant that the role of women caregivers was not diminished, and the reform was used to employ mainly immigrant women or women from the affected families (León and Pavolini, 2014). Indeed, even though the standard provided for exceptional use of a 'family caregiver' (while trying to encourage the use of specialized services), the way in which the law was designed, the crisis, and the lack of funding conspired to boost the family caregiver to predominance (Domínguez-Serrano and Marcenaro-Gutiérrez, 2016).

In any case, some of the measures taken, and above all the evolution of the labor market, allowed the difference between women and men in unpaid working time to move from a multiple of 2.8 to 2.1 from 2002 to 2009, placing Spain among the most equal levels in Southern Europe (though still far from rates in Nordic countries, where the ratio ranges from 1.5 to 1.2) (Charmes, 2015). This lower presence in paid work, together with the gender pay gap mentioned earlier, led to continuation of the pattern where women received 82% of non-contributory pensions in 2007. In terms of these pensions, women exceeded men at pensions worth one and two times the minimum pension, whereas pensions valued at three or more times the minimum were reserved for men (calculations from AEAT data).

The result was that at the end of the expansionary period, Spain presented in terms of social spending when compared to the EU-15 a regression in all areas except widows' pensions and unemployment benefits (given the higher unemployment rate vis-à-vis Europe), this regression being much greater in terms of housing and family. By way of contrast, the areas of education and health presented characteristics like those in the rest of the EU-15 (Muñoz de Bustillo and Antón, 2015).

Secondary inequality of income

The result of all this was that the Gini Index after transfers increased from 31.0 to 31.9 points between 2004 and 2007, as did the 80/20 ratio, from 5.2 to 5.5. Measured after the effect of taxes, the incidence of monetary poverty declined during those same years by 1 percentage point (20.1% to 19.7%).[13] We can thus see that poverty before transfers decreased much more than poverty after transfers, which removes the state as an explanatory factor in the relative improvements in terms of poverty during the final years of the growth period. Indeed, it was the creation of employment that served to moderate trends. However, because job creation came at the expense of containment of the average real wage, it was insufficient to end material deprivation. Although percentages had been declining before the crisis, 27.6% of households still suffered from deficiencies in at least two of the seven concepts usually analyzed,[14] and severe material deprivation still affected 3.5% of households in the year 2007.

In summary, the distribution of income in the period before the crisis was determined by two main factors: on the one hand, changes to the distribution of wealth and capital gains, and on the other, the evolution of employment and wages. The worsening distribution of wealth and the resulting uneven distribution of capital gains generated by the housing bubble help to explain the increasing wealth of the richest individuals. The creation of employment associated with the bubble allowed for some reduction in poverty and limited increases in inequality; however, the lower redistributive capacity of the state and especially the evolution of real wages in a context of permanent adjustment policies prevented any substantial improvement in living conditions. As we shall see, the response to the outbreak of the crisis since 2008 has sharpened the regressive potential of adjustment.

Distribution of income during the period of crisis

The outbreak of the crisis and the impact of the housing bubble had a marked effect on capital gains and wage incomes. Whereas the initial impact of the crisis adversely affected capital gains, new rounds of adjustment policies implemented as early as 2009 concentrated the impact onto employment and wages. The worsening of income inequality and poverty is the result of an unbalanced productive model that maintains business profitability at the expense of the living conditions of a majority of the population.

A reduction in capital gains had begun to take place during 2007, before the GDP of Spain's economy entered a recession. Thus, the importance of capital gains in the income of the top quantiles declined substantially, from representing 42.5% of the income of the richest 1% in 2006 to no more than 9.8% in 2010. This resulted in an initial decline in the share of the top percentiles in gross income before taxes. According to data from the World Top Incomes Database, the share held by the richest 10% declined from its peak of 36.3% in 2006 to 34.7% in 2007 and to 32.5% in 2010.

Analysis of the strategies undertaken since the outbreak of the crisis in this context of declining capital gains reveals that the distributive conflict between capital and labor was situated at the axis of adjustment. However, a simple line of continuity cannot be drawn between these measures and the reforms previously undertaken, because the degree to which they have been applied in recent years has moved them to a qualitatively different level. It is in this context that we must consider the labor counter-reforms lately applied, as discussed in the previous chapter, as well as other reforms that will be dealt with in sections to come (using a structure similar to that previously used).[15] The result has been a direct attack on wages which has consequently increased levels of inequality.

Primary income inequality

Although the crisis initially triggered an increase in average real wages, as a result of the destruction of lower-quality, lower-paid jobs, real wage levels have been practically stagnant since 2009 due to wage adjustments and pressure from the growth of unemployment, all despite low inflationary pressure.

In addition, as seen in Figure 5.5, the wage structure has been homogenized downwards, so that 60% of total wage earners have maximum salaries of just twice the SMI.[16] The segment that has grown most and that represents the highest percentage is low-salary workers, with wages equal to or less than half the SMI. This reflects both the destruction of employment and the growing importance of underemployment caused by the crisis.

Table 5.1 does not reflect a growing wage disparity since the outbreak of the crisis; on the contrary, wage dispersion has been reduced, continuing the path followed during the previous period and remaining substantially below the OECD average. The gender pay gap has also been reduced, after an initial rebound, so that in 2015 it stood at 14.9%, according to Eurostat data. Therefore, one must consider differences among the various types of incomes to understand the rise in inequality since the outbreak of the crisis.

Drawing again on analysis of the functional distribution of income, we find that the differences between wages and profits have become more acute. Figure 5.4 shows that the profit share (after a setback in 2008) grew from 36.2% in 2008 to 37.9% in 2015, to the detriment of the wage share, which fell from 54.6% to 52.9% of total income. Thus, simultaneous with an upswing in inequality levels, the strategy of wage involution pursued since the pre-crisis growth stage continued and intensified to reactivate accumulation.

Taking all this together, one notes that the worsening of income distribution has been a direct consequence of the deepening wage adjustment process. Developments in real wages have increased the incidence of in-work poverty, which affected 13.1% of wage earners by 2016. This, together with the elimination of jobs, has redounded to a worsening of the Gini Index. Calculated before social transfers, it increased from 45.4 points in 2007 to 50.7 in 2016.

Redistribution of the public sector and secondary income inequality

The redistributive capacity of the public sector

In terms of the WS, the first aspect that must be considered is the resource problem that needed to be addressed. On the one hand, between 2007 and 2009 public revenues fell by almost 6 percentage points of GDP (Eurostat data). This fall reflected the weakening tax system during the expansionary era: in a context where public revenues grew, especially via the real estate sector, electioneering tax reforms were implemented that reduced the maneuverability of the public sector when the real estate sector sank. As the International Monetary Fund (2009) pointed out, between 2.5 and 3 percentage points of GDP in public revenues were linked to the construction sector at that stage.

At the same time, public spending rose 7 percentage points between 2007 and 2009. This was the result of multiple factors: the initial application of Keynesian responses by the government (Muñoz de Bustillo and Antón, 2013), and especially the performance of automatic stabilizers, as unemployment increased (whereas other benefit recipients, such as pensioners, continued to grow in number), as discussed in Chapter 3. This explains how between 2008 and 2014, social spending increased from 21.4% to 25.4%, a larger increase for that variable than was experienced by the overall EU-15 (at nearly 3 percentage points, according to Eurostat data).

The increase in the number of recipients of social benefits with the onset of the crisis was staggering, and not only due to unemployment: between 2007 and 2015, the number of unemployment beneficiaries rose from 1.5 to 2.1 million (after falling from 3 million in 2009), and contributory pensions (of all types) rose from 7.7 to 8.4 million, mainly due to retirement (data from the Ministry of Employment and Social Security [MESS]). Between 2007 and 2014 (the most recent available year), the increase in real expenditure per person (both dependent and not dependent on support) was 6.8% in total, or about 400 euros per person, whereas the equivalent increase for the EU-15 was 10.7%. As a result, the process of convergence with the EU-15 in this area was slowed and slightly reduced: at the beginning of the crisis, Spain had a per capita social expenditure of around 57% that of the EU-15; by 2014, that figure was 55.1% (data calculated from Eurostat).

These trends are due to the fact that the increase in benefit recipients took place in a context where intense adjustment measures were being applied that would affect the WS. In line with what has been done by many countries worldwide (Ortiz and Cummins, 2013), Spain has implemented important restrictive policies to its WS, including pension reforms, the healthcare system, and income benefits (see also Álvarez Peralta et al., 2013, pp. 210–217).

With respect to the pension system, among the changes introduced by the 2011 reform was the (gradual) increase in the retirement age from 65 to 67, an increase in the number of contribution years required to collect the maximum pension (from 35 to 37 years), an increase in the number of years counted for the calculation of pension (from 15 to 25), and a hardening of conditions for access to early retirement. Regarding the 2013 reform, pensions were moved from a defined benefit system to a defined contribution system, making it impossible to know in advance the amount of pension to be collected, as this will be adjusted annually according to the level of social contributions (thereby socializing the poor functioning of the labor market) (Banyuls and Recio, 2015).

With regard to the healthcare system, the number of drugs outside public coverage (and therefore available at higher prices) has risen, and a pharmacy co-payment has been introduced to populations who once received these medications at no charge. To this must be added the outsourcing of many services (including the healthcare service itself in certain autonomous communities). In addition, the universality provided by the system from 1986 was *de facto* abolished through restricted access to healthcare, driving out irregular migrants, who can use emergency services only; persons over age 26 without previous contributions; and other groups (Banyuls and Recio, 2015).

The other key provision within the WS is the educational system, and as noted by Banyuls and Recio (2015), certain educational lines have been removed for special-attention groups, such as children with learning difficulties at both primary and secondary levels, as have reinforcement staff. In addition, pre-schools have increased fees and outsourcing to private groups, while at the same time criteria that directly affect service quality, such as student-to-teacher ratios, have become more flexible. In higher education, the ostensible hike in fees has come along with a reduction in scholarships and an increase in the workload of teachers (and the consequent dismissal of staff with temporary contracts). Finally, the educational reform as applied since the crisis began, has introduced changes that go beyond parametric terms, modifying the system by differentiating itineraries according to school performance from an early age (accentuating the inequality of opportunity) through mechanisms of evaluation and selection. The effects that these changes will have on overall inequality in Spain have yet to be seen.

Likewise, progress made in prior years in terms of gender equality has been reversed since the outbreak of the crisis. Improvements introduced in paternity leave were dropped with the first austerity package in 2010, and institutions created to promote gender equality were directly suppressed. The right to miss work for reasons of work/life balance was curtailed in the labor reform of 2012. Finally, the financing of both early childhood (pre-age 3) and long-term care programs (Dependency Law) was significantly reduced. The result has been an intensification of the 'familist' component of the WS, which is to say greater dependence on (unpaid) care work by women and/or social assistance (León and Pavolini, 2014; Alonso and Trillo, 2015).[17]

Finally, the evolution of other income benefits has followed the same downward trend. According to Ortiz and Cummings (2013), Spain before 2013 was already among the EU-15 countries that had implemented measures to target monetary benefits, putting them out of reach for a portion of the population in need. On the other hand, using the OECD Tax-Benefits database, it can be seen how unemployment benefits have suffered significant cuts across all user profiles (some even before the crisis; see Gómez Serrano and Buendía, 2014). Thus, the ability of these provisions to mitigate the risk of income loss associated with unemployment fell by nearly half between 2007 and 2013 (the last year available in the OECD Job Quality Database).

Regarding the effectiveness of this WS, and despite the previously mentioned trends, it improved its capacity to attenuate inequality and poverty. In the case of the former, reduction of inequality improved from 25.3% in 2008 to 31.9% in 2015; with respect to poverty, improvement increased from 47.6% to 53%. Because this appears to contradict what has been said regarding reforms, two explanatory qualifications must be made. First, most of the reduction in inequality was replicated in the rest of the EU-15, whose average value rose from a reduction of 38.7% to 43% during the period indicated. In the case of poverty, something similar occurred, although in a less pronounced way. As Immervol and Richardson (2011, p. 35) explain, due to progressive mechanisms of taxation and social benefits, the marked increases in market income inequality due to rising unemployment (by 25% between 2008 and 2014 in Spain) cause redistributive effects to be increased automatically, even in a context where redistributive policies are not modified (or even when they are tightened). Using the data here presented, it is certainly illustrative that the greatest reductions in inequality occurred in Portugal (by more than 18 percentage points for the 2008–2015 period) and Greece (by 11.7 points).

The second qualification has to do with Figure 5.7. Comparison among the development of EU-15 countries and their redistributive capacities in terms of poverty continues to leave Spain (with Ireland and Italy) in the rear. This, along with what has been said about the evolution of the WS, prevents the prediction of optimistic trends in terms of inequality.

Secondary inequality of income

According to Eurostat data, the share of the top 10% in terms of disposable income increased from 23.6% in 2007 to 24.9% in 2016. Moreover, disposable income increased at an average cumulative annual rate of 2.4% for the ninth and the tenth top deciles from the beginning of the crisis (Figure 5.8). In contrast, the lowest decile's income went down in absolute terms, at an annual rate of 0.7%. Although the remaining deciles saw their total income improve in a certain proportion, all levels below the sixth decile experienced a drop in their shares of disposable income. Under these conditions, it is no surprise that the 80/20 ratio climbed from

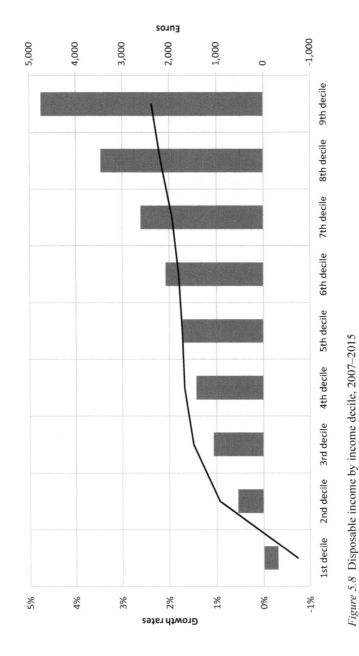

Figure 5.8 Disposable income by income decile, 2007–2015

Note: The variation in available income is calculated as the difference between the top cut-off point in 2015 and 2007 for each of the households' income deciles according to household incomes survey data. Eurostat do not provide that point for the 10th decile.

Source: Own elaboration with data from Eurostat.

5.5 to 6.6 points over the 2007–2016 period, according to Eurostat data, whereas the Gini Index after transfers rose from 31.9 to 34.6 in 2015 (among the worst in the EU, preceded only by Estonia with 34.8, Latvia with 35.4, Bulgaria with 37.0, Romania with 37.4, and Lithuania with 37.9).[18]

If we analyze the data by group, the decline in income in the Spanish economy most affected younger persons, older persons, and non-EU migrants. Whereas the average income per person decreased by 0.4% on average between 2008 and 2015, that of persons aged between 16 and 29 fell by 2.0%, that of persons aged 65 and over fell by 1.6%, and that of the foreign population (from countries outside the EU) declined by 1.3%.[19]

Despite an apparent improvement in the redistributive action of the state, it has been insufficient to compensate for the worsening of income distribution caused by wage adjustments. Ultimately, this has led to a significant increase in the percentage of persons at risk of exclusion and suffering material deprivation. According to the indicator used by Eurostat and the INE, the percentage of persons at risk of poverty or social exclusion went from 23.3% to 27.9% of the population in 2007–2016. The second measure in its narrowest definition (severe material deprivation) meanwhile increased from 3.5% to 5.8% of the population. Here the brutal impact of adjustments on income and the material conditions of life and their link with the wage dimension of income seem obvious.

The distributive pattern prior to the crisis had already exposed the inability of the Spanish economy's growth model to ensure an improvement in the living conditions of the population. Our analysis of what has occurred in terms of income inequality and poverty since the outbreak of the crisis clearly reveals that the continued attack on labor income has been the main vehicle for Spanish capitalism to ensure profitability.

Conclusions

Consistent with the imbalances observed in our analysis of the pattern of accumulation and of the configuration of the Spanish labor market, we have shown that the rise in levels of inequality is not a feature exclusive to the recent recessive phase, but that the growth model deployed in the pre-crisis period precluded improvements in the living conditions of the majority of the population. In fact, despite a rate of economic growth higher than that of the main capitalist powers, poverty levels fell only slightly and remained at levels above those of the EU-15. Moreover, the policy decisions adopted were inclined to direct the fruits of growth towards activities other than improving the capacity of the state to mitigate these trends, including the weakening of the tax system and clearly regressive reforms.

The reactivation of accumulation was based on recovery of profitability through the application of a rigid wage adjustment, explaining the involution of the average wage and the regression of the wage share. Because wage dispersion did not increase during this period, rises in primary income inequality are explained by analysis of the functional distribution of income. Although the creation of precarious jobs concealed the regressive potential of adjustment during the growth phase, its link with worsening living conditions has become evident since the outbreak of the crisis, with the state opting not to influence these trends.

On the other hand, the share of wealth controlled by workers over the period declined, and wage constraints were not compensated by higher incomes derived from ownership of assets, nor from greater participation in capital gains linked to speculative bubbles. Indeed, the higher-income households were the main beneficiaries of this asset revaluation. Hence, the unequal distribution of family assets becomes significant in understanding the greater wealth of segments with higher incomes, especially during the pre-crisis period. Besides, the WS did not become a source for compensation for wage earners, because the fruits of growth were not used to reduce the social protection gap between Spain and the rest of the EU, as measured by its redistributive capacity. Only in some areas did the WS in Spain improve during this period, whereas regressive trends dominated in the rest.

Since the onset of the crisis, the situation has worsened not only because of the recession, but due to the policies adopted to combat it. In fact, the re-establishment of wage adjustment strategies of greater depth resulted in sharper increases in inequality. The superior deciles of income are those that have improved most remarkably with respect to the rest, which experienced regression. Again, functional income analysis reveals that the causes behind the highest levels of inequality can be found in the latent conflict between capital and labor: whereas the share of profits in total income has maintained an upward path in recent years, the wage share has deepened its deterioration. Concerning the WS, despite the increase in its redistributive capacity, which is explained by the role of automatic stabilizers in a context of a terrible economic shock, cost-containment measures have had regressive effects reinforcing its underdevelopment. Attenuation in the levels of inequality will require a departure from dynamics of accumulation subject to the demands of profitability.

Notes

1 Author names are given in alphabetical order, as all share equal responsibility for this chapter.
2 The Bank of Spain (BoS) has published these data since 2002 on a triennial basis. They permit disaggregated analysis of the distribution of wealth.
3 The data are presented in gross and net terms, discounting the value of the debts linked to the acquisition of these assets, with the aim of detecting possible specificities in the indebtedness processes of the salaried class. The separation of data relating to the principal residence from the rest is justified in its consideration as a means of consumption, which provides direct services. Possession does not generate capital gains linked to the speculative bubble: the potential increase in income would be realized only if the asset were sold, which does not allow the majority to employ it as a durable consumer good. If this were done, the effect would be diluted by the increase in real estate prices when buying or renting another home (Cottrell, 1984: 142). Only 2.3%, 4%, and 3.3% of households in 2002, 2005, and 2008, respectively, increased their level of consumption through access to higher levels of indebtedness resulting from increases in the price of their primary residence. In that regard, the main beneficiaries of the real estate bubble were those households that also owned other types of real estate (data from BoS, EFF).

4 We have defined the group of wage-earning households in the EFF as all those in which the reference person claims to have been employed for the better part of his or her working life.

5 Although a portion of the resources deposited in these types of investment is channeled towards public debt, the majority is directed towards private-sector financing, largely targeting the acquisition of different titles of social ownership.

6 Capital gains include income from the sale of real estate assets and financial assets. Therefore, this type of income does not include income generated by such assets, including rents or dividends (which are considered part of the capital income).

7 It should be recalled that the main source of income statistics on the wealthiest persons is the fiscal data and, specifically, the personal income tax. According to the definition offered by authors who have treated such data for the World Top Incomes Database, from which the series for our analysis were obtained, the concept of income is 'gross income before all deductions and including all types of income declared in personal income tax: wages and pensions, net income from entrepreneurial activities, dividends, interest, other investment income, and other types of minor income [as well as] realized capital gains'.

8 The sharp decline in the following year (Figure 5.3) is in line with the increase in new unsold housing, which rose from 273,000 to 414,000 properties between 2006 and 2007, thus relating these incomes to the housing bubble.

9 We used as indicators for this analysis wages and profits, defined in both cases in relative terms (*WS* and *PS*). Each reports the relative share of each of these types of income over total income and is obtained as follows:

$$WS = CE \: / \: National \: Income = CE \: / \: GDPfc \: (1)$$
$$PS = GOP \: adjusted \: / \: National \: Income = GOP \: adjusted \: / \: GDPfc \: (2)$$

where *WS* = Wage Share; *CE* = Compensation of Employees; *GDPfc* = Gross Domestic Product at factor cost; *PS*: Profit Share; *GOP*: Gross Operating Surplus.

For the *PS* calculation, an adjusted version of *GOP* is used. *A priori* the most appropriate method to analyze the effect of the functional distribution of income on personal income inequality would be using net operating surplus, which is calculated by discounting the depreciation of fixed assets from the *GOP*. However, the typical use of accelerated amortization strategies for fiscal purposes causes the risk of distortion of the analysis; thus, we have chosen to use *GOP* as a reference indicator.

The National Accountancy imputes in the *GOP* the income of the self-employed. We have deducted it assuming that the income received by a self-employed person corresponds to the average real wage.

By dividing both the numerator and the denominator of the expression (1) by the total number of wage earners (*L*), we obtain the factors on which *WS* evolution depends. Specifically, this can be defined as the relationship between the average real wage and the productivity of wage earners:

$$WS = (CE \: / \: L) \: / \: (GDPfc \: / \: L) = Average \: real \: wage \: / \: Productivity \: of \: wage \: labor \: (3)$$

10 Both options avoid bias caused by the use of the number of employees due to the increasing weight of part-time employment. Figures have been obtained from the authors' own calculations based on data from the National Institute of Statistics (in Spanish, INE) and AMECO.

11 The crisis has had a severe impact on the country's public accounts since the end of 2008 (and especially in 2009), which is why in this part of the analysis we regard 2008 as the turning point.

12 Given statistical availability, we have had to observe for measures of inequality the period 2005–2016 (although for Spain, the first set of data is from 2004).

13 The INE offers two indicators of poverty rates: the at risk of poverty or social exclusion (AROPE) rate as measured per criteria established in the Europe 2020 Strategy,

and the INE's own measurement. The former reduced from 25% to 23.3% and the latter from 20.1% to 19.7% during the period 2004–2007.

14 These concepts are as follows: 'Cannot afford to go on vacation at least one week a year'; 'Cannot afford a meal of meat, chicken, or fish at least every other day'; 'Cannot afford to keep the house at an adequate temperature'; 'Unable to cope with unforeseen expenses'; 'Has had to delay the payment of expenses related to the primary residence (mortgage or rent, gas receipts, etc.) in the last 12 months'; 'Cannot afford to own a car'; and 'Cannot afford a personal computer'.

15 Data from the EFF end in the year 2011, so it will not be possible in this section to analyze the evolution of distribution of wealth during the post-crisis period.

16 In the case of the self-employed, by the end of 2015, the percentage of self-employed workers meeting the minimum base had increased to 86.1% of the total.

17 Unfortunately, the last survey conducted on differences in time use between men and women was that of the INE for 2009–2010, which impedes the incorporation of these data (see European Commission, 2013: 112).

18 When making comparisons, we have maintained 2015 as the reference year because no data are available for most countries in 2016.

19 Authors' own calculations based on data from the INE Living Conditions Survey.

References

Alonso, N. and Trillo, D. (2015): 'La crisis del estado de bienestar y sus repercusiones sobre la situación sociolaboral de las mujeres', *Revista de Economía Crítica*, 20, pp. 135–154.

Álvarez, I., Luengo, F. and Uxó, J. (2013): *Fracturas y crisis en Europa*, Madrid: Clave Intelectual.

Banyuls, J. and Recio, A. (2015): 'Crisis dentro de la crisis: España bajo el neoliberalismo conservador', in L. Steffen (ed.), *El triunfo de las ideas fracasadas. Modelos de capitalismo europeo en la crisis*, Madrid: La Catarata, pp. 39–69.

Charmes, J. (2015): 'Time Use Across the World: Findings of a World Compilation of Time Use Surveys', *Background Paper*, New York: UNDP Human Development Report Office.

Cottrell, A. (1984): *Social Classes in Marxist Theory*, London: Routledge.

Del Rosal, M. and Murillo, J. (2015): 'Acumulación y crisis en la Eurozona', in Juan Pablo Mateo (coord.), *Capitalismo en recesión*, Madrid: Maia, pp. 137–175.

Domínguez-Serrano, M. and Marcenaro-Gutiérrez, Ó.D. (2016): 'Cuidados a mayores y menores en Andalucía: mucho camino por recorrer', in L. Gálvez Muñoz (dir.), *La economía de los cuidados*, Sevilla: Deculturas.

European Commission (2013): *The Impact of the Economic Crisis on the Situation of women and Men and on Gender Equality Policies*, Luxembourg: Publications Office of the European Union.

Gómez Serrano, P.J. and Buendía, L. (2014). *La crisis y los Estados de bienestar en Europa*, Madrid: Fundación FOESSA. Available at: http://foessa2014.es/informe/uploaded/documentos_trabajo/15102014153256_1506.pdf

Gutiérrez, R. (2014): 'Welfare Performance in Southern Europe: Employment Crisis and Poverty Risk', *South European Society and Politics*, 19 (3), pp. 371–392.

Immervoll, H. and Richardson, L. (2011): 'Redistribution Policy and Inequality: Reduction in OECD Countries', *Working Papers (OECD Social, Employment and Migration)*, 122.

International Monetary (IMF) (2009): *Spain: Selected Issues*, Washington, DC: FMI.

León, M. and Pavolini, E. (2014): ' "Social Investment" or Back to "Familism": The Impact of the Economic Crisis on Family and Care Policies in Italy and Spain', *South European Society and Politics*, 19 (3), pp. 353–369.

Moreno, L. (2001): 'La "vía media" española del modelo de bienestar mediterráneo', *Papers: Revista de Sociologia* (63–64). Availale at: www.raco.cat/index.php/Papers/article/view/25608

Muñoz de Bustillo, R. and Antón, J.I. (2013): 'Those Were the Days, My Friend: The Public Sector and the Economic Crisis in Spain', in D. Vaughan-Whitehead (ed.), *Public Sector Shock. The Impact of Policy Retrenchment in Europe*, Cheltenham: Edward Elgar Publishing, pp. 511–542.

———. (2015): 'Turning Back Before Arriving? The Weakening of the Spanish Welfare State', in D. Vaughan-Whitehead (ed.), *The European Social Model in Crisis Is Europe Losing Its Soul?*, Cheltenham: Edward Elgar Publishing, pp. 451–506.

Navarro, V. (2006): *El subdesarrollo social de España*, Barcelona: Anagrama.

Ortiz, I. and Cummins, M. (2013): 'The Age of Austerity: A Review of Public Expenditures and Adjustment Measures in 181 Countries', *Working Paper (Initiative for Policy Dialogue and the South Centre)*.

Rodríguez Cabrero, G. (2011): 'The Consolidation of the Spanish Welfare State (1975–2010)', in A.M. Guillén and M. León (eds.), *The Spanish Welfare State in European Context*, Surrey: Ashgate, pp. 17–38.

Conclusions

Spain's lost decade

Luis Buendía and Ricardo Molero-Simarro[1]

Having analyzed in previous chapters the various elements that illuminate the links between the expansive phase for Spain's economy and the crisis that began in 2008, we now draw certain conclusions and finish with remarks concerning the future prospects for the country.

Our analysis shows that the reaction to the profitability crisis that arose in Spain was an adjustment on wages, in which the economic structure played a crucial role. Although we have highlighted the logical sequence of crisis and wage adjustment, we also find that the strategies of capital proved a major factor in productive developments over the last decade. Thus, do we examine the power constellation in order to understand the forms adopted during adjustment.

Although the housing bubble was not a direct cause of the wage adjustment, it was indeed capital's answer to its own profitability crisis, and here the role played by financial capital cannot be disregarded. Both financial and construction capital became the core of Spain's growth model due to expectations of greater profitability in a general context of productive stagnation. In this, capital counted on further aid from a public sector with which it had historically developed close links. Significantly, this took place in a context of European integration that allowed for a decline in interest rates even greater than the drop in profit rates, leading to the appreciation of real estate assets. The accumulation process was thus conditioned and productivity came to a halt. At the same time, total material requirements and the discharge of polluting residues increased, given that the accumulation process was highly demanding in ecological terms.

Since the interruption of the accumulation process, when the real estate bubble burst, the contradictions within Spain's economy have been dealt with through deeper structural adjustments. However, these adjustment policies have not served to modify either the economy's accumulation model or its dependent external insertion in the context of membership in the Economic and Monetary Union (EMU). During the expansive phase, foreign capital had increased its presence in the main capital-intensive manufacturing branches. Nevertheless, the technological content of Spanish exports remained low, and this has continued to be the case since the advent of the crisis.

Despite an improved current account balance during recent years, exports still lack sectorial and technological diversification. Geographical diversification is also low, with the European Union (EU) as the principal trading partner, and it is here that Spain's trade profile shows its main weaknesses. The country's export share remains stagnant at around 1.7%, and far from increasing competitiveness, internal devaluation policies have enhanced the dependent specialization of the Spanish economy.

Meanwhile, labor market reforms were introduced, aimed at achieving internal devaluation, deepening the trend followed during the expansive phase, and making jobs more precarious, even while the relative wage declined. First of all, labor market deregulation has made job precariousness the norm. In fact, the standardization of precarious contractual forms during the period of economic growth facilitated dismissal without cause, as well as non-renewal for a significant number of workers, even before the start of the massive job-shedding process that further affected permanent full-time workers. In addition, labor reforms have permitted contracts signed since 2013 to offer lower wages, worse conditions, and fewer rights, which is to say lower levels of employment protection, in numbers too low to catch up with employment levels prior to the crisis. In other words, the quality of recently created employment has been much lower, due not only to the use of existing precarious contracts but also to the use of new forms, including so-called 'false' self-employment[2] and persons needing to work more than one job.

All of this has had a negative impact on real wages, which remain far from pre-crisis levels. Consequently, the wage share of the national income has clearly gone down, starkly contrasting trends in the core Eurozone countries, where it has increased. However, this specific trend in Spain has not been sufficient to initiate a process of sustained accumulation, even though business profits have increased.

Moreover, as was the case in Latin America, and as explained in the Introduction, foreign financial capital also played a role in these developments. To Spain's traditional financial dependency (related to the liberalization of international financial markets) was added the challenge of European integration. Specifically, Spain's membership into the Eurozone made available vast amounts of cheap credit for Spanish banks and businesses, and this was mainly allocated to the construction and services sectors, at the expense of industrial investment. Although public debt was substantially reduced during the growth period, when the bubble burst there was a transfer of private losses to the government balance sheet, executed through a decrease in public-sector revenues and an increase in expenditures triggered by automatic stabilizers and financial bailouts. This led to the introduction of fiscal austerity measures.

These policies have also affected the social protection system. It should be recalled that the Spanish welfare state never completed its catching-up process vis-à-vis the other EU-15 countries. Quite the contrary: despite certain relevant improvements during the expansive phase (mainly targeted toward fighting gender discrimination), when the crisis hit, Spain was still an underdeveloped welfare state in comparison to other OECD countries; despite this, Spain became the object of new cost-containment reforms. Since 2008, austerity measures have worsened this situation. In effect, a wrong diagnosis concerning the financial sector became a problem for the public-sector accounts, and public debt in 2016 remained at 100% of GDP. Consequently, adjustment policies have been strongly reinforced as a consequence of financial market pressures, only partially compensated for by intervention from the ECB. In this way, adjustment, already applied in the expansive phase through the labor market and reforms of other segments of the welfare state, has become a permanent feature, due to the failure of austerity measures to foster economic recovery.

Wage adjustment policies and austerity measures (public spending cutbacks) have had a significant negative impact on living conditions for Spain's population. Despite the fact that during the expansive phase, the economy grew at a higher pace than elsewhere in the Eurozone, poverty levels in Spain fell only slightly, remaining above the EU-15 level. A fragile tax system and regressive welfare state reforms contributed to this trend. Since the onset of the crisis, the situation has worsened, due not only to the impact of the crisis itself but also to policies adopted to address it. On the one hand, deeper wage adjustment has made primary inequality greater; on the other, the erosion of the welfare state has limited the capacity of public policies to improve income distribution, to redress the unfair gender share of care work, and to guarantee better living conditions in general.

In sum, both the crisis and its management in Spain have clarified the links between productive stagnation, external dependency (in productive, trade, and financial terms), financial imbalances, and worsening work and living conditions for most people (regardless of nationality). This deterioration has been a consequence of the permanent wage adjustment, through which the structural problems of Spain's economy have been addressed. While those problems were partially hidden behind economic growth and job creation during the real estate bubble, the impact of the crisis and the expansion of previous policies have made deep economic and social imbalances in Spain more evident.

Consequently, the outcomes of our research show that the adjustment policies imposed by the Troika are merely strengthening the economy's low-productivity growth model and the dependent pattern of external insertion already in effect before the crisis. In this sense, the optimism shown in the wake of certain macroeconomic figures cannot be supported by the economic fundamentals (much less so, if we also consider the social implications). As we shall explain in detail later, the impacts on the labor market remain hugely negative, magnifying the existing problems of temporariness and structural unemployment, and income inequality is rising above already high levels. In addition, while financial capital has been bailed out, public spending cuts as a response to the debt crisis served first to deepen the recession, then to negatively affect living conditions, increasing the incidence of poverty.

A new social as well as political crisis has emerged in Spain, although the responses to adjustment policies remain fragmentary. New parliamentary forces born in the context of the struggle against austerity remain far from government, except at the local level, where some new public policies that attempt to mitigate the worst effects of the crisis and the management thereof are being tested, but no relevant political force is currently able to challenge the overall process of adjustment. Even if left-wing parties achieve victory in the national government, the experience of Syriza in Greece casts doubts on the real capability of parties to revert the adjustment process in the context of the EMU, although policies applied by the Portuguese coalition of socialists, communists, and Bloco de Esquerda are encouraging.

Considering the similarities between policies implemented in Latin American economies during the 1980s and 1990s and early 2000s and those now being put into practice in Spain, it is possible to assert that wage adjustment is a useful lens through which to understand current developments. First, spending cuts and deregulation measures have slowed the pace of recovery. However, adjustment should not be viewed as merely a wrong (ideological) answer to economic crises. On the contrary, as already noted, adjustment should be understood as a class-biased strategy to restore profitability by means of opening new spaces for private accumulation and by reducing wages in all their dimensions (direct, indirect, and deferred) at the expense of social rights and living conditions.

At the same time, despite the worldwide scope of adjustment policies and the involvement of international financial institutions in their formulation, domestic political, economic, and social forces have played the main role in their implementation. In Spain, the key decision-making position of a trio of actors (government, financial capital, and the construction sector)[3] has been reinforced and continues to shape the growth model.

In this way, the Spanish economy is currently facing its own 'lost decade'. Since the introduction of austerity policies in May 2010, the crisis only deepened, decoupling economic growth in Spain from that in the Eurozone and thus generating a double-dip recession. Despite the gradual recovery since the end of 2013, GDP at the end 2016 remained at its 2010 level. Something similar can be said of labor market indicators: unemployment rates are now lower (in part due to decreased activity rates caused by the discouraged-worker effect, the emigration of qualified young people, and the return of women to home care activities), and the government is quick to boast of the creation of a million jobs between 2015 and 2016, but employment is still below its 2010 level.

Meanwhile, labor reforms have led to an increase in the number of working poor, which along with cutbacks to social benefits, have made Spain one of the most unequal countries in the EU. At the brink of GDP recovery, almost one-third of the population remains at risk of social exclusion, and a relevant share also suffers from severe material deprivation. Should the economy continue on its path of recent years – which is what the Troika proposes when asserting that adjustment in Spain is still 'incomplete',[4] – Spain's 'lost decade' may well turn into a 'lost generation'.

Measures taken since the Partido Popular assumed government in June 2016 (with the support of the right-wing liberal party Ciudadanos and the abstention of the Socialist Party) seem to point at such a future for Spain.

First, the recent bankruptcy of Banco Popular in June 2017 (then the sixth-largest bank in Spain in terms of assets) has shown that the financial crisis was not restricted to quasi-public savings institutions, but that the entire banking system took an active part in the deployment of the real estate bubble. The bank's sale (for €1) to Spain's biggest bank, Banco Santander, in a process promoted by both national authorities and the EU, was the crowning touch in a process of financial concentration that has seen no equal in the EU. This sale will make transformation of Spain's productive model all the more difficult. Unsurprisingly, the few big private banks that dominate the financial landscape in Spain have a relevant interest in the recovery of the real estate market. In fact, housing prices are again increasing faster than the EU average, and housing rents, boosted by tourism and new forms of speculation, are skyrocketing.

Second, the Budget Stability Law, passed in 2012 to develop the 2011 constitutional reform, has introduced new cutbacks to public expenditures despite the gradual recovery in productive activity. Under the EU's excessive deficit procedure still affecting Spain, those cutbacks are the result of progressive reduction of the ceiling for government expenditures; pressure on regions (responsible for most public services) to reduce their own deficits in turn; and pressure on local governments to prevent them from directing fiscal surpluses toward anything but debt repayment, despite their having already met target levels in many cases.

Third, even as the European Commission insists on the need for Spain to apply stronger labor reforms, employers are using their advantageous position in collective bargaining (stronger than ever since the 2012 reform) to reject wage increases, despite improvements in their profits. The resulting deterioration in labor income (suffered particularly by youth, women, and immigrants) explains the social security deficit (and thereby the risk to public old-age pensions), as well as the weak recovery in household consumption. In addition, this helps explain the worsening primary distribution of income and its negative effects on social cohesion in a country with an underdeveloped welfare state.

The continuation of this adjustment pattern is also worsening the structural stagnation and the external and financial dependency of the Spanish model of accumulation. In order to confront the negative effects of adjustment, it would be necessary to introduce transformative policies that address Spain's structural problems and its current social disorder. Many limitations arise as a consequence of membership in the Eurozone, but if an alternative economic program is not introduced to change the fundamentals of the economic model, not only will future crises become more frequent, but social and political deterioration might escalate to unbearable levels.

In this book, we have sought to verify the interrelation of the various dimensions of Spain's economic model. Any attempt to change this model should therefore adopt measures that apply to all these dimensions. We believe that such change is possible only through measures including (but not limited to):

i) The creation of a public-sector bank, the basis of which could be BFA-Bankia, already nationalized. This could reduce the degree of concentration of the financial system but also ensure that growth is channeled towards transformation of the productive model, thus improving its technical profile and guaranteeing its environmental sustainability (especially but not exclusively in terms of energy).

ii) The expansion of public-sector housing, for which the stock currently under the control of the SAREB 'bad bank' could serve as a starting point. In this way, a supply of affordable housing that contributes to meeting the constitutional right to housing could be mobilized, also working to dampen current increases in prices and rents.

iii) The creation of an industrial and research policy that contributes to the transformation of the production model, thereby improving the external insertion of the economy.

iv) The repeal of the 2011 constitutional reform and its subsequent Budget Stability Law in order to reverse the cutbacks to public expenditures made during recent years.

v) The introduction of integral tax reform that helps to increase public revenues in an equitable way. This should guarantee the sustainability and expansion of the welfare state, for instance, through improvement of the socially (and gender) relevant Dependency Law.

vi) The repeal of the labor reforms and old-age pension reform so that a new framework of labor relations can be introduced. This should guarantee the stability and quality of employment, as well as increases in real wages and income benefits (old-age pensions, unemployment benefits, parental benefits, etc.) to improve the currently regressive pattern of income distribution.

All these measures should go hand in hand with a gradual increase in direct and/or indirect public control over strategically relevant economic and business sectors, as well as the spread of cooperative forms of ownership and self-management throughout the rest of the productive and financial system. Only such an increase in the degree of economic democracy would guarantee the preservation of economic and social rights in opposition to the public and private actors that have controlled the evolution of Spain's economy for decades.

Notes

1 Author names are given in alphabetical order, as both share equal responsibility for this chapter.
2 This refers to wage earners who are formally considered self-employed in order for the employer to save on hiring costs.
3 Interestingly, two of these three actors (all but the government), as well as other key Spanish companies, took part in the so-called Business Council for Competitiveness (in Spanish, *Consejo Empresarial de la Competitividad*), created in 2011 and ended in 2017 after having reached its main goals aimed at influencing policy making.
4 'La economía española sigue sufriendo desequilibrios', 26 November 2015, *Expansión*. Retrieved from: www.expansion.com/economia/2015/11/26/5657036c22601df55 38b4594.html (Last accessed on 12 September 2017).

Index